# PATHWAY
# TO
# A
# BREAK OUT
# LIFE

# Pathway
# To
# A Break Out
# Life

MOVE FROM BREAKTHROUGH TO BREAK OUT AND
EXPERIENCE THE LIFE GOD HAS PREPARED FOR YOU

## Dr. Dorri Burrell

**Ingenuity®**
**HOUSE**
**Publishing**

*Cover Design by JB Design Concepts, Houston, Texas*

**Pathway To A Break Out Life**
Move from Breakthrough to Break Out and Experience the Life God Has Prepared for You

ISBN: 978-0-578-61427-4

Ingenuity House Publishing
Spring, TX 77373
ingenuityhouse@gmail.com
www.ingenuityhouse.com

# DEDICATION

*This book is dedicated to my mother, Mary Bruce, who transitioned to be with Jesus on September 16, 2016. She loved reading and writing. She especially loved reading the Bible and self-help books, which also happens to be my favorite as well. I love and miss you so much. Thank you for instilling in me to always be and do my best.*

# TABLE OF CONTENTS

# ACKNOWLEDGMENTS

A special thanks go to my loving husband, Apostle Barry Burrell, who also happens to be my pastor and my best friend. You are an awesome man of God and have always been there to encourage me even in the difficult times. Thank you for utilizing your computer skills in helping me assemble this book. I will love you forever.

A heartfelt thanks must also go to my mother-in-law, Pearl Burrell, (my honey bunny), who I love so dearly. I appreciate all your prayers and inspiration. Every time you told me you wanted the first copy of my book, I became more determined to hurry up and complete it. Well, here it is!

Thank you to my sons, Joshua and Jeremy who lovingly tell me I can do whatever I need to, and make me feel like I am the best while doing it! You have always had my back and I will always be available for you. I love you two with all my heart.

Thank you to my daughter-in-law, Ashley, for all the warfare you rendered on my behalf and the love you have shown towards me. You are the best daughter-in-law ever! Thank you for my beautiful granddaughters, Emily and Jewel, who always warms my heart.

I extend much gratitude to the Living Water Family, especially those who prayed daily on the prayer line from 12 noon to 1pm for the completion and success of this book. Living Water, you all are the sheep I prayed for and have now manifested. May God richly bless you.

Much appreciation is given to Rodney Cash, my son in the Lord. Truly I was inspired every time we spoke and you told me about the different books you were writing. I became more and more determined to pen my thoughts. Finally, my book is complete. Much success on your books. Love you much!

Dr. Melba Adams, I truly appreciate the love you've shown me throughout the years. Thank you for your assistance in editing this book. May God bless you tremendously.

Thank you to everyone who prayed and pushed me until this book was completed. I water the seeds of greatness inside each of you and speak blessings in your lives.

Many thanks to Prophetess Yolanda Banks, owner of Ingenuity House Publishing. Thank you for having so much confidence in me along with your consistent encouragement. Thank you as well for the design and production of this book. Your graphics are unmatched.

# INTRODUCTION

Have you ever asked someone how they were doing, and they responded, "I'm blessed and highly favored"? Their lives appeared to be filled with victory. They didn't seem to have a problem in the world, so you decided to start saying it as well. Now, when someone asks you how you are doing, your energetic reply is, "I'm blessed and highly favored!" It sounds good and you are really trying not to doubt that this is true for you, but what in the world is going on? You've been to every breakthrough service, every prophetic conference, every anointed oil service, yet there is still an element of victory missing from your life. When I say victory, I am not talking about the acquisition of things, I'm talking about an internal victory that brings external results. Things happen to be a by-product of this victory. If the above person sounds like you or someone you know, then prayerfully this book will be a great tool of deliverance.

About eighteen years ago I was the person in every church service. When I say every service, I mean every service, and we had church seven days a week. I was the prayer and praise leader, but my life still lacked the success and freedom I'd read about in the Word that others seemed to be walking in. I kept wondering, "Lord when is it going to be my time?" I'd gotten breakthrough after breakthrough, but something was still missing. One day I decided to start spending more quality time with God, and as I did this, day after day, year after year, not only did I breakthrough but I broke out of everything that had been defeating me for years. I broke through, which means I moved beyond what had been holding me back. After I broke through, I broke out, meaning, never turned back by becoming violent in the spirit though my obedience to God! I am no longer getting delivered from the same thing over and over, but now I am FREE! When Jesus frees you, you are free!

I have written this book for people who are serious about being totally free. This book is designed to provoke the reader do a self-examination and prayerfully decide that now is the time to break through and break out of everything that has been sent to bind, hinder or restrict you. God wants you to walk in the freedom he has already given through his Son Jesus Christ. This is an awesome opportunity God is presenting. Take advantage of it, break through and break out, through the pathway of successful living through Christ.

# PATHWAY
# TO
# A
# BREAK OUT
# LIFE

# CHAPTER ONE

# So Loved

John 3:16 - For God so loved the world that he gave his only begotten Son, that whosoever believeth in him should not perish but have everlasting life.

For anyone who has ever been rejected or abandoned, this Scripture should be a real encouragement. You are "so loved." Have you ever taken time to meditate on those words? The Hebrew translation of the word "meditate" is to mutter. Mutter means to say something over and over. We mutter alright, but it is usually words of negativity; nobody loves me, nobody cares, or I'm not good enough, and the list goes on and on. The truth is, all those statements are lies. You are "so loved" with all your shortcomings, mistakes, mishaps, and failures. God, the creator of heaven, earth and the universe took time out of his schedule to think about you. He devised a plan for you to have everlasting life. God showered you with love when he sent his only son Jesus to receive many stripes so you could be healed when you get sick. He allowed Jesus to be beaten, bruised, abused and rejected just for you. He allowed Jesus to carry your sins to Calvary. God's love flows freely, and it has brought you life everlasting. Everlasting life will not be anything like this life here on earth. There will be no sorrows, woes, heartaches or pain. There will be nothing but love and absolute beauty: a sea of glass, gates of pearl, and an angelic choir singing "Holy, Holy, Holy." God loves you! He has plans for you. As a matter of fact, he is thinking good and peaceful thoughts about you right now. He has a hope and an awesome future for you. (Jer. 29:11 AMP) He knows how to right every wrong in your life. You haven't had a relationship until you have been in a relationship with God. You haven't been loved until you have been loved by God.

You don't have to worry about who does not love you, or who abandoned you because God's love is unending, and he will never leave you. You will leave him before he leaves you! He loves you just that much! Isn't that good news! Oftentimes we are used to the kind of love that takes, but the love of God gives. He gives us joy during times of sorrow. He gives us hope when all seems hopeless. He gives us encouragement when life says we can't. He tells us to live when we feel like dying. He makes life worth living!

God's love is unconditional, incomprehensible and transforming. No matter where you are and what you are doing, God's love can find you. In the book of St. John, the fourth chapter, we find Jesus leaving Judaea to go to Galilee. He did not travel the usual route. He was determined to get to Galilee by way of Samaria. As he passed through Samaria he stopped in Sychar where Jacob's well was located. By this time, it is about the sixth hour (12 noon) and Jesus is very tired, so he stops at the well to take a rest. As he was there a woman comes to the well. This is unusual within itself for a woman to come to the well to draw water at this time of day. The other women drew water early in the morning or evening when it was cool. Perhaps this lady was trying to draw more than water! I'm just saying!!! Although it seemed she was there at the wrong time, it was the right time. Little did she know that this was the day she would be transformed by love. She was a Samaritan and Jesus was a Jew. They were two races of people who had nothing to do with each other. When it comes time for Jesus to show you how much he loves you, it doesn't matter who or where you are, he is going to pour it on. He is not prejudiced. His love flows to all races, creeds and colors.

As Jesus begins to converse with this woman, she is amazed that he has spoken to her. Jesus asks her for a drink of water which sparks this response:

*John 4:9* - Then saith the woman of Samaria unto him, How is it that thou, being a Jew, askest drink of me, which am a woman of Samaria? For the Jews have no dealings with the Samaritans.

Little did she know this was going to be a conversation that would literally change her life. Jesus was there for her. Jesus came to meet a natural woman and take her to a spiritual place she had never been before. She was used to people treating her a certain way, but this would be the first time someone was coming to her to add to her life rather than take away. Jesus is love, and love gives. Jesus responded to her question by telling her:

*John 4:10* - If thou knewest the gift of God, and who it is that saith to thee, Give me to drink, thou wouldest have asked of him, and he would've given thee *living water*.

She was baffled at Jesus' response. What was this water to be drawn with, and not only that, where was this *living water* that would cause her to never thirst again? She tells Jesus:

*John 4:15* - Sir, Give me this water, that I thirst not, neither come hither to draw.

She expressed to Jesus that she wanted this *living water* he was talking about. Although she was asking, Jesus wanted to know how bad she really wanted it so he proceeded to tell her to go get her husband. At this point Jesus was about to lavish her with a love she had never known before, a deep, nonjudgmental, unconditional, transforming love.

*John 4:16–18* - Jesus saith unto her, Go call thy husband and come hither. The woman answered and said, I have no husband. Jesus said unto her, Thou hast well said, I have no husband: For thou hast had five husbands; and he whom thou now hast is not thy husband: in that saidst thou truly.

She was amazed to find out that Jesus, a man she did not know, knew all about her. Without judgment, he told her her personal business, which was a little embarrassing. Because of the love Jesus showed this woman, her perception was opened. She knew he was different from all the other men she'd met.

*John 4:19* - The woman saith unto him, Sir, I perceive that thou art a prophet.

Now that she knows who Jesus is, she quickly changes the subject lest Jesus tells her more about herself. She begins to talk about worship, and where her fathers worshiped. She is a pretty fast talker, but she cannot out talk Jesus. He has an answer for everything she brings up. His answer shuts her down every time until eventually she realizes he is more than a prophet; he is the Messiah! She throws down her waterpot and goes into the city yelling:

*John 4:29* - Come, see a man, which told me all the things that ever I did: is not this the Christ?

From this point on the Samaritan woman was never the same. The encounter she had with Jesus at the well changed her life. She went to draw water, but she received a taste of living water that transformed her life through the love that was poured out.

Jesus saw beyond this woman's actions in life. He saw her soul that had been wounded and crushed by life. He didn't judge her because of her previous actions: he brought healing to her wounded, fragmented soul. She was so excited that she did not keep this encounter quiet. She went into the city proclaiming Jesus' goodness!

Just as Jesus showered his love on this Samaritan woman, he wants to do the same for you. He is gracious, forgiving, and merciful. No matter how anyone else judges you, what they say about you, or how they feel about you, it cannot stop the transforming love of Jesus Christ. Whatever your issue is, open up and be honest with God. Let him love away the negativities of yesterday, shining a light on today, so you can live a brighter tomorrow.

YOU ARE SO LOVED!!!!

# Prophetic Word

Thus saith the Lord, I have loved you with an everlasting love. When you were a thought in my mind, I loved you. When you did things that were displeasing in my sight, I loved you. When you drifted away from me, I still loved you. I loved you so much that I orchestrated events that would cause you to once again call upon my name. My love and kindness were extended towards you and you were drawn back to me and served me even greater. Look to me, saith God. Seek me like never before, for I desire to manifest myself to you in a greater way. There are many facets to me, says God, and I want you to know me with more than a surface love. Go deeper into my Word. Study like never before. There are jewels I want to reveal to you. The more you study my Word, the more I will impart into you. I want my love to flow through you like liquid. When people speak with you, I want them to feel my love flowing that they may be drawn to me. Did I not say, "If I be lifted up, I will draw all men to me?" Lift me up, says the Lord! Lift me up! I want you to be a conduit of my love; a love that saves, heals, forgives and delivers. The world is filled with so much darkness, so go forth as lights shining the light of love everywhere you go, saith the Lord your God!

# Power Scriptures

**Romans 5:8**
But God commendeth his love toward us, in that while we were yet sinners, Christ died for us.

**I John 4:19**
We love him, because he first loved us.

**I John 4:10**
Herein is love, not that we loved God, but that he loved us, and sent his Son to be the propitiation for our sins.

**Jeremiah 31:3**
The Lord hath appeared of old unto me, saying, Yea, I have loved thee with an everlasting love: therefore with lovingkindness have I drawn thee.

**John 15:13**
Greater love hath no man than this, that a man lay down his life for his friends.

**I John 4:9**
In this was manifested the love of God toward us, because that God sent his only begotten Son into the world that we might live through him.

## I John 4:16

And we have known and believed the love that God hath to us. God is love; and he that dwelleth in love dwelleth in God, and God in him.

## II Thessalonians 3:5

The Lord direct your hearts into the love of God, and into the patient waiting for Christ.

## Psalm 143:8

Cause me to hear thy lovingkindness in the morning; for in thee do I trust: cause me to know the way wherein I should walk; for I lift up my soul to thee.

# Reflections/Notes

_____

_____

_____

_____

_____

_____

_____

_____

_____

_____

_____

_____

_____

_____

_____

_____

_____

_____

_____

_____

_____

_____

_____

_____

_____

_____

CHAPTER TWO

# Love Gives, Lust Takes

L ove! Do we really know what love is? Is it that tingly
feeling you get when you are with your significant
other? Is it getting everything you want? Is it being told
what you want to hear? Is it never having to be challenged on
your thoughts or ideas? Is it being so consumed with someone
else that you can't sleep at night?

Contrary to what we have been taught, love is none of
the above. Love isn't just a feeling, it's action. God's love caused
him to act. His action was GIVING! True love gives. When
you truly love someone, giving is automatic. Giving, not in the
sense of "stuff" but a giving of yourself. Giving patience when
it seems you have no more to give. Being kind not only when
you feel like it, but mostly when you don't. Love suffers long,
which means you have the ability to put up with some things

for a while. Love is not irritable, which means everything doesn't get on your nerves. When you really think about it, you probably get on others' nerves as well! We can all work on loving more by monitoring our thoughts and learning to respond rather than react. There is a difference between the two. Reacting is acting without thought, but responding is thinking before you act. Love responds, not reacts.

Lust and love are polar opposites. Lust takes! Lust always says, "What can you do for me?" Lust looks to be fulfilled. It does not seek to fulfill the needs of others. How does lust sound? You can hear it spoken loudly in the words I, me, my and mine because lust is selfish. It is always seeking ways to get what it wants without consideration of how others will be affected.

Lust does not come from God. Lust is Satan's counterfeit of love and it comes in many forms. It is not just extreme sexual desire, it also includes excessive desire for things, power, positions, money, etc. As believers we do not have to lust after anything because God is the god of provision. When we begin to lust, we are not trusting God and are walking on Satan's territory.

Satan loves to toy with people's minds through planting thoughts that are contrary to the word of God. He knows if those thoughts are received then your actions will change from godly to ungodly. When your actions change he sits back and watches the demise. When a lustful thought comes to mind, do not meditate on it. The Bible tells us what to do with negative thoughts.

*II Corinthians 10:5* - Casting down imaginations, and every high thing that exalteth itself against the knowledge of God, and bringing into captivity every thought to the obedience of Christ;

Every ungodly thought should immediately be expelled from our minds and replaced with a corresponding Scripture. What we meditate on is what we become. In the Old Testament God told the children of Israel to keep the Word as frontlets before their eyes. (Deuteronomy 11:18) He was telling them to keep the Word in view. Even if your mind forgets it, your eyes will see it and bring it to your remembrance. Every lustful thought must be cast down!

Lust has brought many powerful people to their demise, believers as well as unbelievers. God hates lust and does not want it found in the lives of those who are called by his name. If we say we are believers, we should *believe* God to deliver us from everything that is not like him that would cause a breach in our relationship. God tells us what to do about lust.

*I John 2:15-17* - Love not the world, neither the things that are in the world. If any man love the world, the love of the Father is not in him. For all that is in the world, the lust of the flesh, and lust of the eyes, and the pride of life, is not of the Father, but of the world. And the world passeth away, and the lust thereof: but he that doeth the will of the God abideth forever.

God tells us not to love the world, nor anything in it. He spells out the three forms of lust: lust of the flesh, lust of the eyes and the pride of life which the world thrives on. Many television or billboard ads are filled with sexual images because the advertisers know those images will catch people's eyes. It might also catch your eye, but you must know how to turn away quickly. The world along with all its lust will eventually pass away, but those who do the will of God will live forever.

Lust of the flesh is doing things we should not do in order to gratify the flesh. Apostle Paul tells us how to overcome the flesh.

*Galatians 5:16-17* - Walk in the Spirit, and ye shall not fulfill the lust of the flesh. For the flesh lusteth against the Spirit, and the Spirit against the flesh: and these are contrary the one to the other: so that ye *cannot* do the things that ye would.

Lust of the eyes is looking at anything that incites lust. We can look at something with admiration, but when it goes beyond admiration it is time to turn away. In II Samuel 11:2, David should have turned away when he saw Bathsheba bathing on the rooftop. Instead he kept looking until he burned with lust. He sent for her, even after he knew she had a husband and proceeded to fulfill his lustful desire upon her.

*II Samuel 11:2*-3 And it came to pass in an eveningtide, that David arose from off his bed, and walked upon the roof of the kings house: and from the roof he saw a woman washing herself: and the woman was beautiful to *look* upon. And David sent and enquired after the woman. And one said, Is this not Bathsheba, the daughter of Eliam, the wife of Uriah the Hittite?

You have to know when to stop looking! The more you look, the more lust is stirred up, and what started out as admiration has now turned into lust, which is a sin. Don't be guilty!

Last but not least is the pride of life. God hates pride. Since God hates pride, we should as well. Pride is what brought Satan down. Pride promotes self-exaltation. God tells us how to get exalted in I Peter 5:8.

*I Peter 5:8* - Humble yourselves therefore under the mighty hand of God that he may exalt you in due time.

The godly way to exaltation is through humility. Isn't that a paradox! God's ways are not our ways, and his way is the best way. Humble yourself, and let God exalt you. When God exalts you, no man can bring you down!

We cannot love God and the world which is full of lust. In the book of Joshua, Joshua tells the Israelites, who had fallen into idolatry, to choose who they would serve, God or idols. Both cannot be served; there must be a choice. Joshua made it clear that he was going to serve God. We must make a choice. There is no fence straddling. We are either on one side or the other.

Lust left unchecked is like a wildfire. It gets completely out of control. In II Samuel 13, a young man by the name of Amnon burned in lust for his stepsister, Tamar. He had a wicked friend who devised a plan for his desires to be fulfilled. Amnon pretended to be sick and asked his father, King David, if Tamar could make him some cakes and feed him. Nothing sounded wrong about this request, so David agreed. Tamar went to Amnon's house, made the cakes and proceeded to feed him. Amnon, in his wickedness, put everyone out of the room except Tamar. While Tamar was feeding him, he told her to lie with him (as in physical intimacy). Tamar was appalled by his request but was unable to keep him from committing this dastardly deed.

*II Samuel 13:14*-15 Howbeit he would not hearken unto her voice: but, being stronger than she, forced her, and lay with her. Then Amnon hated her exceedingly; so that the hatred wherewith he hated her was greater than the love wherewith he had loved her, and said unto her, Arise and be gone.

Lust caused Amnon to literally rape Tamar, his own half-sister. How horrid!

Aside from the physical damage, how much devastation must that have caused in her soul? His selfishness caused her more pain than he could ever imagine but he didn't care. After raping her he told his servants to put her out and bolted the door after her. He treated her as though she was the perpetrator. Tamar was inconsolable. She put ashes on her head, threw off her garment of many colors that represented her virginity, put her head in her hands and cried, cried, cried.

Lust caused Amnon to be a taker which caused terrible repercussions in his life. Two years later he was killed by his half-brother Absalom. What a sad story! Unfortunately, stories like this are still happening today. Lust has an insatiable appetite and it is one of the most detrimental tools Satan uses to bring people down daily.

Do not allow lust to linger in your spirit. If you can't stop looking at pornography, you are feeding the spirit of lust. If you are looking at music videos full of lasciviousness, you're feeding the spirit of lust. If your head turns one hundred and eighty degrees when a nice-looking person walks by, you're feeding the spirit of lust. If a lustful thought comes to mind and you don't cast it down, you are feeding the spirit of lust. Remember, whatever you feed grows.

There are many more examples I could give, but you get the picture. Don't feed lust, ask God to free you. Don't pet lust, ask God to deliver you. Lust is a taker, so see it for what it is! Don't let it take holiness from you. A little lust is a big demon waiting to manifest and cause destruction. God does not want his people walking in lust or lusting after anything.

Lust should not be a part of our lives because it is not a part of God. God wants his people to live godly and holy lives. If you have a problem with lust, be honest with yourself and God. Now is the time to get delivered. God loves you and he still heals and delivers (sets free)! Don't be too embarrassed to allow God to deliver you. Be embarrassed to continue walking around with lust in your heart. God is speaking in love today. Surrender!!!!! Surrender to the Word of God that will bring freedom to your soul. Noted below is a good Scripture to aid in your deliverance.

*Psalm 119:9-12* - Wherewithal shall a young man [or woman], cleanse his [or her] way? by taking heed thereto according to thy word. With my whole heart have I sought thee: O let me not wander from thy commandments. Thy word have I hid in mine heart, that I might not sin against thee. Blessed art thou, O Lord: teach me thy statutes.

Deliverance comes through taking heed or paying attention to the Word of God. Paying attention does not mean to look at only, but it means to DO! It doesn't mean to *just* Do, but to DO IT with your WHOLE HEART. Give it all you've got; all your mind, all your will and all your emotions. Hide the Word in your heart so when the enemy puts a thought in your mind it will be negated because of what is in your heart. Let God know you are serious. He will send you grace to help in time of need. Your deliverance is nigh.

Remember, love gives, lust takes. Don't let it take from you anymore. Now is the time of salvation.

LOVE GIVES! LUST TAKES!

# Prophetic Word

My love gives, saith the Lord. My love never takes. My love caused me to make the ultimate sacrifice which was the life of my Son. I watched as he was beaten, battered, lied on and rejected, but this was all in my plan of giving. I loved the world, in its evil and wickedness, so much so, that I gave my only Son, Jesus, that whoever will believe in him does not have to perish but will receive everlasting life. That is love! Love is not seeing how much someone can do for you, but how much you can do for them. Love is not seeing how much someone can give you, but how much you can give to them. Love will cause you to sacrifice. Love will sometimes cause you to be uncomfortable so someone else can be comfortable. Love does not manipulate, lie and scheme. That is lust! Love does not control. That is lust! Love seeks not its own. That is lust! Lust is what caused David to take the wife of Uriah, one of his most valiant men. Lust is what caused Amnon to rape Tamar. Don't be a taker, saith the Lord. That is not part of my character, neither should it be part of yours. Be a giver! Love gives! All will know you are my disciples by the love you show to one another, by your ability to bless those who curse you, and pray for those who use you. My love gives! Lust takes! Give! Give! Give, saith the Lord thy God!

# Power Scriptures

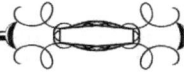

### I Corinthians 13:4-8
Charity suffereth long, and is kind: charity envieth not: charity vaunteth not itself, is not puffed up, Doth not behave itself unseemly, seeketh not her own, is not easily provoked, thinketh no evil; Rejoiceth not in iniquity, but rejoiceth in the truth; Beareth all things, believeth all things, hopeth all things, endureth all things. Charity never faileth:

### Proverbs 6:25-26
Do not lust in your heart after her beauty or let her captivate you with her eyes. For by means of a whorish woman a man is brought to a piece of bread: and the adulteress will hunt for the precious life.

### Galatians 5:16
This I say then, Walk in the Spirit, and ye shall not fulfill the lust of the flesh.

### Romans 8:8
They that are in the flesh cannot please God.

## James 1:13-15

Let no man say when he is tempted, I am tempted of God: for God cannot be tempted with evil. But every man is tempted, when he is drawn away of his own lust, and enticed. Then when lust hath conceived, it bringeth forth sin: and sin, when it is finished, bringeth forth death.

# Reflections/Notes

_____

_____

_____

_____

_____

_____

_____

_____

_____

_____

_____

_____

_____

_____

_____

_____

_____

_____

_____

_____

_____

_____

_____

_____

_____

_____

_____

_____

_____

_____

# CHAPTER THREE

# Worry

The Bible has much to say about worry, mainly, do not do it! Worry changes nothing and robs us of precious time that could be spent in productivity. Worry is a thief and must be treated as such. Would you welcome a burglar into your home, sit back and watch him take what he wanted? I'm sure your answer is "no!" Well, we must be just as adamant about not allowing worry to take root in our soul and govern our lives. Rather than worry, let's see what Jesus tells us in the Sermon on the Mount:

*Matthew 6:25* - Therefore I say unto you, Take no thought for your life, what ye shall eat, or what ye shall drink; nor yet for your body, what ye shall put on. Is not the life more than meat, and the body than raiment?

As Jesus teaches, he gives us many life principles, and if adhered to we will be extremely successful. In this Scripture Jesus is saying, "Do not worry about your life," specifically, what you will eat, drink, or wear. One of the greatest temptations ever is to worry about ourselves. Will I ever be happy? Will I have enough money to do the things I need to do? Will my children or spouse ever receive Christ? Will my business ever be successful? We can always worry about something, but we should never worry about anything.

Worry has never changed one situation. The only way a situation can change is to do what you can and give the rest to God. How do you know when you've handed it to God? You have handed it to God when you can walk in peace, totally trusting him to work it out. Peace is one of the benefits of the believer. Jesus was speaking to his disciples in preparation for his earthly departure, and one of the things he told them he was giving them was peace. He did not want them to worry or be fearful about anything.

*John 14:27* – Peace I leave with you, my peace I give unto you: not as the world giveth, give I unto you. Let not your hearts be troubled, neither let it be afraid.

We are Jesus' disciples, so the same words he spoke to the twelve applies to us. Jesus did not just tell them he was leaving them peace, he said he was leaving *his peace*. What is the difference between *peace* and *his peace*? Peace is when you have found a place of rest in the midst of a trial, then something else comes along, shakes you up and peace evades you. Jesus' peace is different. It is a peace that cannot be shaken or disturbed: it is steadfast no matter what. You no longer toss and turn while your mind races one hundred miles per hour. You say your prayers, go to bed, and go to sleep! God gives his beloved sweet sleep. (Psalm 127:2)

When we spend time worrying we are walking contrary to the will of God. He does not want us carrying burdens. He is our burden bearer.

*I Peter 5:7-8* - Casting all your care upon him; for he careth for you. Be sober, be vigilant; because your adversary the devil, as a roaring lion, walketh about, seeking whom he may devour:

When we worry we are giving the devil an invitation to come in and bring more trouble into our lives. He is constantly trying to find ways to bring us mayhem and destruction. We can always walk in victory over him by being vigilant in our obedience to God. We have to cast, *throw,* our cares to the Father in prayer, who always has a listening ear for his children. We must have an intense knowledge of how much he cares for us and know he already has things worked out in our lives.

II Chronicles 19-20, tells us of a young man by the name of Jehoshaphat, the king of Judah, who walked in the ways of the Lord, and the Lord was with him. He made sure the Word of God was taught throughout his territory.

The people of Judah brought him presents, and he had riches and honor in abundance. Jehoshaphat was doing well until he became friends with the most evil king around, King Ahab. Ahab convinced Jehoshaphat to join him in battle against Ramoth-gilead. This was not Jehoshaphat's battle, and needless to say, he almost got killed. He came to his senses, cried out to God, and God helped him. (II Chronicles 19:31) God spared Jehoshaphat although he was angry with him for joining himself with an ungodly king. When Jehoshaphat returned home, God sent a prophet by the name of Jehu to give him a message.

*II Chronicles 19:2* - And Jehu the son of Hanani the seer went out to meet him, and said to King Jehoshaphat, Shouldest thou help the ungodly, and love them that hate the Lord? therefore is wrath upon thee from before the Lord.

God allowed numerous enemies to come against Judah and Jehoshaphat *became afraid.* He began to **WORRY!** He knew his actions had brought trouble to his territory. Instead of allowing worry to *linger,* he began seeking the Lord, and proclaimed a fast throughout all Judah. He knew exactly what to do. We should follow his example when trouble comes our way, even if we brought it upon ourselves. We have to know how to cut worry off! Don't embrace it! Cut it off! Don't pet it! Cut it off! Don't let it linger! Cut it off! Cut it off through prayer and fasting. As all of Judah stood before the Lord with their little ones, their wives, and their children, Jehoshaphat lead a very anointed prayer. He prayed until the presence of

God filled the place. The Spirit of the Lord came upon a prophet by the name of Jahziel who proclaimed the following message to Jehoshaphat and the congregation.

*II Chronicles 20:15-17* - And he said, Hearken ye, all Judah, and ye inhabitants of Jerusalem, and thou king Jehoshaphat, Thus saith the Lord unto you, Be not afraid nor dismayed by reason of this great multitude; for the battle is not yours but God's. Tomorrow go ye down against them: behold, they come up by the cliff of Ziz, and ye shall find them at the end of the brook, before the wilderness of Jeruel. Ye shall not need to fight in this battle: set yourselves, stand ye still, and see the salvation of the Lord with you, O Judah and Jerusalem: fear not, nor be dismayed; tomorrow go out against them: for the Lord will be with you.

In this prophetic word, the first thing God tells the king and the people is not to be afraid or dismayed. In other words, DO NOT WORRY! God reassures them that he will fight for them and gives them directions. After he gives them directions, he tells them again, don't fear or be dismayed. In other words, DO NOT WORRY! As it turns out, just like God said, Jehoshaphat and the people of Judah did not have to fight at all. The only weapon they had to use was their mouths. Jehoshaphat appointed singers and told them to say, "Praise the Lord; for his mercy endureth forever." I'm sure he didn't choose those who were going to sing in their heads. I'm sure he didn't choose those who were going to sing like they were singing a lullaby. He needed some radical praisers who did not mind opening their mouths and belting out, "Praise the Lord; for his mercy endureth forever!" As they began to sing, and praise, the Lord sent ambushments against their enemies and they were slaughtered. Hallelujah!

Suppose Jehoshaphat had allowed worry to consume him rather than fasting, praying, and getting everyone in his kingdom to do the same thing? They would have been defeated. There is no victory in worry! God does not want us worrying. He wants us to trust him in every situation and circumstance. He wants us to cry out to him in prayer, receive and follow his instructions, believing that he has already worked things out. He wants us to keep our eyes on him no matter how our situation looks. This is all part of our faith walk.

*II Corinthians 5:7* - For we walk by faith and not by sight.

Walking by what we see can be very discouraging. What we see tells us there is no way out and we might as well give up. We should allow ourselves to be encouraged by what David said in the book of Psalms:

Psalm 23:1 The Lord is my shepherd; I shall not want.

We must allow God to be our shepherd. We must know he is a loving, caring shepherd who prides himself in taking care of his sheep. He does not want us up all night trying to figure things out. He is the one who doesn't slumber or sleep: he wants us to sleep like a baby! He doesn't want us anxious or intimidated by anything because he is an omnipotent God. He is all powerful and he is our Father! He does not want us stressed out. When we are worried, stressed out, and filled with anxiety, we are telling God we don't need his help because we are working things out ourselves. Don't worry! Relax! Breathe! God is God! Cast your care upon him because he can handle anything and everything. The time is now to STOP WORRYING!

# Prophetic Word

Thus saith the Lord, Worry not. I am your God. Trust me to move on your behalf. I am your maker and I am concerned about everything that concerns you. Do not worry but pray to me. Prayer shakes loose those chains of worry that would come to bind, restrict, and keep you from seeing through the eyes of faith. Faith is what the enemy is after. Be mindful of his tactics and schemes and do not fall into his traps. Worry is a trap! When you worry you are listening to the voice of the enemy and not mine. My voice tells you to stand strong in me. My voice reminds you of who you are to me and the lengths I will go through to fight for you. Give me your every burden. Give me your every care. Cast them on me, saith God. My ears are attentive to your prayers, not the voice of worry that echoes from your soul. Did not I open the Red Sea for Moses and the children of Israel so they could cross over on dry land? Did not I shut the mouth of the lion when Daniel was in the lions' den? I have moved for others: I will move for you. Trust me with all your heart. When the enemy comes to bring fear to your mind so he can set up residence in your soul, close the door. Close the door through speaking my Word. Speak my Word until it becomes more alive to you than anything. As you begin to do this you will be infused with strength from on high, my strength that will cause you to be able to handle any situation, saith the Lord thy God.

# Power Scriptures

### Philippians 4:6-7
Be careful for nothing; but in everything by prayer and supplication with thanksgiving let your requests be made known unto God. And the peace of God, which passeth all understanding, shall keep your hearts and minds through Christ Jesus.

### I John 5:14-15
And this is the confidence that we have in him, that, if we ask anything according to his will, he heareth us:
And if we know that he hear us, whatsoever we ask, we know that we have the petitions that we desired of him.

### Hebrews 10:35
Cast not away therefore your confidence, which hath great recompence of reward.

### Proverbs 12:25
Heaviness in the heart of man maketh it stoop: but a good word maketh it glad.

### Psalm 56:3
What time I am afraid, I will trust in thee.

## Psalm 56:11

In God have I put my trust: I will not be afraid what man can do unto me.

## Psalm 55:22

Cast thy burdens upon the Lord, and he shall sustain thee: he shall never suffer the righteous to be moved.

## Joshua 1:9

Have not I commanded thee? Be strong and of a good courage; be not afraid, neither be thou dismayed: for the Lord thy God is with thee whithersoever thou goest.

## Hebrews 11:1

Now faith is the substance of things hoped for, the evidence of things not seen.

# Reflections/Notes

_____
_____
_____
_____
_____
_____
_____
_____
_____
_____
_____
_____
_____
_____
_____
_____
_____
_____
_____
_____
_____
_____
_____
_____
_____
_____

# CHAPTER FOUR

# Strength

Strength is developed through the struggles we go through. Nobody I know really enjoys and is signing up for struggles, but facing challenges head on builds strength. Often we find strength we didn't know we had through choosing not to buckle in the midst of adversity. There was a time in my life when I did not know how to handle difficulty and emotions ruled my life. I'd pray and cry, and cry and pray, but...the cry was a pity cry, a woe is me cry. There was no faith to be found in those tears. One day while feeling sorry for myself because of the trials that had come my way, I picked up my Bible and came across a Scripture that revolutionized my life:

*Proverbs 24:10* - If thou faint in the day of adversity, thy strength is small.

When I read those words, it was as if the lights were turned on. This Scripture hit me like a ton of bricks. God was telling me I was a WIMP! I had him, his Word, Jesus, the Holy Spirit, angels, the anointing, and I was fainting (giving up) because of trials, tribulations, and circumstances. We must realize we have a choice when trouble knocks on our door. We can choose to answer in faith with the Word, or just listen to the knocks, allowing fear to take residence in our souls. I did not like the fact that God told me I was weak. It was embarrassing and it hurt, but I definitely knew **GOD** was not lying, neither was he revealing this information to hurt me. I'm sure he was tired of seeing me being pitiful rather than the overcomer he knew he made me to be. Needless to say, those words propelled me to action. Every time I had an opportunity to show weakness, I would hear the above Scripture in my mind. I began to allow it to propel me beyond every negative and weak feeling in my soul. I became a doer of the Word and began to manifest the promises it entailed. My tears began to dissipate, my eyes became brighter and my smile became real. No longer did I see adversity as automatic defeat, but as an opportunity to flex my spiritual muscles by operating in strength through Christ and not my own. My own strength is limited, but Christ's strength has no limitations or boundaries!

*Philippians 4:13* - I can do all things through Christ which strengtheneth me!

The strength of Christ is available for us anytime and anywhere. We must take advantage of it and draw from it.

Anything neglected will die. If we neglect to draw from the strength of Christ, we will experience more defeats than ever before because our strength will run out. There is an old adage which says, "After you have tried everything else, try Jesus." I beg to differ. Try Jesus first and you will save yourself heartache, mayhem, sadness, and sorrow. God will also grace us every day, and the more we realize that the easier life becomes. Grace is God's unmerited divine assistance. We don't deserve it! We can't earn it! He supplies us with it daily, and it will carry us through any situation we encounter as long as we look to him.

We should never forget the fact that we have an enemy who is constantly plotting our demise. He constantly seeks ways to cause us to fail. He studies us to find our weaknesses, or buttons, so he can not only push them but lay on them. He so badly wants us to fail.

*I Peter 5:8* - Be sober, be vigilant; because your adversary the devil, as a roaring lion, walketh about seeking whom he may devour.

The Word has instructed us to be sober and vigilant which means we should be sharp in the spirit and recognize the tactics, schemes, and craftiness of our adversary.

We should be aware that he is always trying to deplete our strength which depletes our faith. Our faith is what he is after. He knows that without faith we are a displeasure to God. He is a displeasure and he wants us to be the same, BUT he is a LIAR!

We must make sure we don't look like a lamb chop when the adversary looks our way. Refuse to be devourable. He wants to devour us, our faith, hope, and dreams. Don't give him what he wants! He is a thief! Don't be a blessing to a thief. This thief comes for three reasons. Let's take a look at the following Scripture.

*John 10:10* - The thief cometh not, but for to steal, and to kill, and to destroy: I am come that they might have life, and that they might have it more abundantly.

Satan works diligently to steal our faith. He is very subtle and cunning. The best thing about him, is that he has already been defeated by our Lord and Savior Jesus Christ! Christ whipped him on Calvary over 2000 years ago! Hallelujah! Since he has already been defeated, he should never win any battle he wages against us. We must know who our Father is, and who we are in him. When those facts are solid in our spirit during the times our strength is being challenged, we don't fall apart, or pull away from God, but we begin to draw closer to God.

*James 4:8* - Draw nigh to God, and he will draw nigh to you...

How do we draw nigh, or closer to God? We do it through prayer. God is waiting to hear our voices reminding him of his promises; not that he needs to be reminded, he wants to see that we are reminding ourselves. Sometimes when we encounter difficulty after difficulty it can wear us down mentally. Satan loves to play tricks with our minds, especially when we are worn down. We must remember to put him under our feet where he belongs! When we remind ourselves of what God has told us, we experience an infusion of faith which will cause us to flex our spiritual muscles and stand strong in him. We know we cannot fail because we are trusting in him and not limiting our unlimited God. We are never alone no matter what we go through. The one who is greater than all difficulty, hardship, misfortune, or disaster that can ever come our way lives on the inside of us. Hallelujah!

*I John 4:4* - Ye are of God, little children, and have overcome them: because greater is he that is in you, than he that is in the world.

We can live as overcomers if we remember who lives, resides and abides on our inside. We can live in the "greater" because the "Greater One" lives in us. When we are weak, he is strong, and his strength is made perfect in our weakness. (II Corinthians 12:9) There will be times in all our lives when it looks like we will not make it, but we must not focus on the trial, we must focus on the one who will carry us through the trial. In Mark chapter 4 after Jesus finished teaching the multitudes by the seaside, he told his disciples:

*Mark 4:35* - ... Let us pass over unto the other side.

That sounded like a good idea. They'd been with Jesus as he was teaching, now he is finished, and it is time to leave. Little did they know that a great storm was on the way. So it is with us, sometimes things are going well: our family is fine, things are great on the job, bills are paid and we even have a little nest egg saved up. Then all of a sudden something happens and our world is shaken. As the disciples and Jesus were traveling to the other side a great storm arose. The wind was boisterous, and the waves were rough. Jesus was in the hinder part of the ship ASLEEP. The disciples were not asleep or sleepy: they were frantic. How could Jesus sleep at a time like this? When they could no longer take it, they woke Jesus up and asked him:

*Mark 4:38* – Master, carest thou not that we perish?

Sometimes when we are in adverse situations it may seem as though God does not care about us and we are perishing. Thank God, he does love us! We don't live by what we see in the natural, or our feelings; we live by faith, or at least we should. Our feelings will lie to us and tell us we are not going to make it, but our faith will tell us we have already made it. Our faith will remind us to lift up our eyes unto the hills from whence cometh our help, and that our help comes from God. (Psalm 121:1-2) He will not allow us to perish and he is always with us. The disciples forgot who was with them, JESUS! Not just another man, but the one who had cleansed the leper, healed the sick, and raised the dead. Oftentimes we, like the disciples, forget who is in the storm with us. We forget previous miracles he has given us. We used to sing a song entitled, "Jesus I'll Never Forget What You've Done for Me," yet there are still some storms that can rattle our soul. Jesus does not want us to fall apart in adversity. He was disappointed with the disciples when they were petrified during the storm. He did not pet them. He was perturbed, which is the same way he feels about us when we behave in a similar manner.

Jesus proceeded to rebuke the wind and speak to the sea.

*Mark 4:39* – And he arose, and rebuked the wind, and said to the sea, Peace, be still. And the wind ceased, and there was a great calm.

Jesus was showing the disciples and us how to handle difficulty. He wants us to use our CREATIVE ABILITY and SPEAK! He is showing us, that some things need rebuking, and other things need to be spoken to. Jesus rebuked the wind, but he spoke to the sea. He rebuked the wind because it was causing a disturbance to everything and everyone. He knew once the wind was under control everything else would follow suit. He spoke to the sea commanding it to be at peace, because it too was reacting to the wind. The effects of the wind caused a spiritual uproar in the disciples which caused Jesus to rebuke them. They'd seen Jesus handle many adverse situations on numerous occasions, now it was their time to do what they'd seen done, but they failed the test. When tribulation comes our way, we must not collapse. We must remember the creative

43

power we have been endowed with by the Father and begin to open our mouths and speak victory in the midst of negativity. This pleases God and he will back us up!

*Isaiah 57:19* - I create the fruit of your lips...

If you want to get God excited and yourself renewed, start speaking words of victory so God can start creating. Either he will change the situation, or he will change you in the situation. Remember, you are already a winner! Thanks be to God who always causes us to triumph through Jesus Christ our Lord! (I Corinthians 15:57)

Father, I draw strength from you, and your supply is unending!

# Prophetic Word

Thus saith the Lord, Be strong in me and in the power of my might. My strength never runs out. What you cannot do on your own you can do through me. I will empower you as you go forth. Do not allow what you go through to weaken you. Draw strength from me and I will cause you to conquer every obstacle that comes your way, whether internal or external. Life can throw some blows that will try to knock the wind out of you, but remember that the Greater One lives on your inside, and greater is he that is in you, than he that is in the world. I am stronger than any principality or power, for I am ALL POWERFUL. Do not be afraid of the fiery darts that are thrown your way. Hold on to your shield of faith. Have faith in me, my Word, and my ability to do anything except lie or fail. You are not alone, so do not fear. I will strengthen you. I will help you. I will uphold you with the right hand of my righteousness. Lift up your heads, O ye gates, and the king of glory shall come in. Who is the king of glory? The Lord strong and mighty! The Lord mighty in battle! The Lord of Host is my name! Do not be afraid for I have already gone before you and VICTORY has already been declared, saith the Lord God Almighty!

# Power Scriptures

### Psalm 73:26
My flesh and my heart faileth: but God is the strength of my heart, and my portion forever.

### Isaiah 40:29
He giveth power to the faint; and to them that have no might he increaseth strength.

### Isaiah 41:10
Fear thou not; for I am with thee: be not dismayed; for I am thy God: I will strengthen thee; yea, I will help thee; yea, I will uphold thee with the right hand of my righteousness.

### Psalm 31:24
Be of good courage, and he shall strengthen your heart, all ye that hope in the Lord.

### Philippians 4:13
I can do all things through Christ who strengthens me.

### I Corinthians 10:13
There hath no temptation taken you but such is common to man: but God is faithful, who will not suffer you to be tempted above that ye are able; but will with the temptation also make a way of escape, that ye may be able to bear it.

## Psalm 22:19

But be not thou far from me, O LORD: O my strength, haste thee to help me.

## Psalm 25:1-3

Unto thee, O Lord, do I lift up my soul. O my God, I trust in thee: let me not be ashamed, let not mine enemies triumph over me. Yea, let none that wait on thee be ashamed.

# Reflections/Notes

# CHAPTER FIVE

# I'll Do It Later

I'll do it later. Many of us have said these very words and later still haven't arrived. Later became later and later, then later became never. There is a word for that, and it is called procrastination. Procrastination is putting off for tomorrow what should be done today! We've left many jobs undone and many deadlines unmet because of telling ourselves these words, "I'll do it tomorrow, or I'll get it done later." Tomorrow is not promised to us, so we must do what we can while we can.

When someone tells us they are going to do something, and they fail to do it, we become disgruntled. We even go so far as to call them a liar. We say out of our own mouths, "They shouldn't have told me they were going to do it if they weren't going to." Oftentimes we require more from others than we require from ourselves. We lie to ourselves all the time by saying we are going to do this or that, and never do it. We don't call ourselves liars. We don't even feel bad about it. We keep giving ourselves chance after chance. We must begin to hold ourselves accountable as much as we would someone else. We must also give others the same mercy we expect them to show us.

*Matthew 5:7* – Blessed are the merciful: for they shall obtain mercy.

Procrastination also causes us to miss many opportunities. In Genesis chapter 6, during the time of Noah, God had grown weary of all the wickedness, corruption and violence in the land. People were doing whatever came into their minds. When God could no longer tolerate their behavior, he decided to destroy everything on earth. Noah was different from everyone else. He found grace in God's eyes which caused the lives of him and his family to be spared. Let's take a look at Genesis.

*Genesis 6:17-18* – And behold, I, even I, do bring flood waters upon the earth, to destroy all flesh, wherein is the breath of life, from under heaven; and everything that is in the earth shall die. But with thee will I establish my covenant and thou shalt come into the ark, thou, thy sons, and thy wife, and thy son's wives with thee.

God gave Noah numerous specific instructions and he followed them verbatim according to Genesis:

*Genesis 6:22* – Thus did Noah according to all that God commanded him, so he did.

Noah had to do what God said in the time allotted. What if he had dragged his feet on building the ark and gathering the animals? What if he had waited for people to agree with him? What if he'd waited until he felt like building the ark? He could have rationalized the instructions given him by God and missed the salvation of his family, himself and the precious animals God wanted to save. That would have been disastrous! Thankfully Noah worked diligently in obedience to God and received salvation because of it. How many wonderful things do we miss out on because of procrastination, and how many other people are affected because of it?

Have you ever asked yourself, "Why do I procrastinate?" That is a good question to ask. When asking that question, you have acknowledged that there is a problem. What one denies, he is not willing to change. Change is not easy, but it is possible. We find it easy to procrastinate because most of us have been doing it all our lives. It is a bad habit that has not been dealt with, but now is the time. Some of the reasons we procrastinate are:

1. We have a lack of confidence.
2. We don't want to commit to what it takes to do it.

3. We are lazy.
4. We are letting time manage us instead of us managing time.
5. We have agreed to do something we did not want to do. (for all the people who have not learned to say "NO")
6. We are afraid of failing.

In order to walk in the success God has ordained for our lives we must be honest with ourselves and change our mindset. Through observation I have noticed that people do what they want to do, whether good, bad, helpful or detrimental. Whatever we decide to do, we do, so we should decide to do what we need to do and eliminate all excuses, relieving ourselves from the bondage of procrastination which brings assassination to our goals. We must stop allowing ourselves to fall short. Now is the time to demand more of ourselves.

God does not want us walking in procrastination which is the breeding ground for failure. He did not create us to be failures. There is another character in the Bible named Lot who almost missed what God had for him because he procrastinated. Lot was told to get his family and leave Sodom because it was about to be destroyed due to its wickedness. Lot shared this information with his sons-in-law who thought he was out of his mind. When the time of departure was at hand angels came to encourage him to *quickly* gather his family and leave.

*Genesis 19:15-16* - And when the morning arose, then the angels hastened Lot, saying, Arise, take thy wife, and thy two daughters which are here; lest thou be consumed in the iniquity of the city. And while he lingered [procrastinated], the men laid hold on his hand, and upon the hand of his wife, and upon the hand of his two daughters; the Lord being merciful unto him: and brought him forth and set him without the city.

Lot lingered [procrastinated] and the angel picked up Lot, his wife, and his two daughters and brought them out of the city so they would not be consumed. God was so merciful to Lot that he sent angels to bring him and his family out. Abraham had prayed for God to spare Lot and God kept his promise even during Lot's slothfulness and procrastination. We must know when to get in a hurry. Time is not promised to anyone and we must do what we can while we can. We must LOVE NOW! We must FORGIVE NOW! We must start that BUSINESS NOW! We must WRITE THAT BOOK NOW! We must say YES TO GOD NOW! Whatever assignment God has given us we must DO IT NOW! Tomorrow isn't promised and we must live each day like it is our last!

*Psalm 90:12* - Teach us to number our days, that we may apply our hearts to wisdom.

Wisdom says, "DO IT NOW!" Write a to-do list and DO IT NOW! Fulfilling the list will require intense focus. If you are one who is easily distracted, deprive yourself of this luxury. There is no time for distractions. You can control yourself!

*Proverbs 25:28* – He that hath no rule over his own spirit is like a city with broken down walls.

*Galatians 5:22-23* – But the fruit of the Spirit is love, joy, peace, long-suffering, gentleness, goodness, faith, meekness, TEMPERANCE [self control], and faith.

Don't wait any longer. Discipline yourself.

In Ecclesiastes 6 we are admonished to consider the ways of the ant which does everything it needs to do without a guide, overseer or ruler. Let's be as wise as an ant. Today is the day to start doing what you said you were going to do tomorrow. Tomorrow isn't promised.

Do It NOW! Do It NOW! Do It NOW! Your rewards are already prepared!

# Prophetic Word

THUS SAITH THE LORD, DO IT NOW!

# Power Scriptures

**Proverbs 13:19**
The desire accomplished is sweet to the soul: but it is an abomination to fools to depart from evil.

**Romans 14:12**
So then every one of us shall give account of himself to God.

**Proverbs 18:9**
He that is slothful in his work is brother to him that is a great waster.

**Ecclesiastes 3:1**
To everything there is a season, and a time to every purpose under the heaven:

**Ephesians 4:26**
Be ye angry, and sin not: let not the sun go down upon your wrath.

**Proverbs 13:4**
The soul of the sluggard desireth, and hath nothing: but the hand of the diligent shall be made fat.

**Proverbs 14:23**
In all labor there is profit: but the talk of the lips tendeth only to penury.

**Proverbs 20:4**
The sluggard will not plow by reason of the cold; therefore will he beg in harvest, and have nothing.

# Reflections/Notes

_____

# CHAPTER SIX

# Using Time Wisely

Some years ago my husband and I visited a fellow parishioner at the hospital. She'd been sick for quite a while. As a matter of fact, at the time of our visit she was in ICU. Before entering her room we had to put on a mask, gown, shoe coverings and gloves. I remember the feeling of uneasiness I had when I began to put on those garments, as I had never experienced that before. When we entered her room, we noticed she kept turning her head from left to right as if in a struggle. We called her name, but she rendered no response. We are not sure if she knew we were in the room or not, but at that time whatever was going on with her had nothing to do with us. After we'd been there a few minutes, still turning her head from left to right, clenching the covers, she yelled out, "But Lord, I haven't done all you told me to do!" We didn't realize she was dying. Nurses immediately came into the room and started working on her but to no avail. She lived her final few moments in a struggle and trying to bargain for more time. That scenario has never left my mind. I have vivid images of those moments as if they just happened and it has been at least 20 years ago.

You are probably saying, "Why would she share a story like that?" I am sharing this story to bring about an awareness to how we are using our time. Every day we wake up we all have the same twenty-four hours, and when it is time to stand before God, we will have to account for how we utilized our time. When our time is up, it is up, unless God extends his grace towards us as he did Hezekiah. Hezekiah was extremely sick and about to die. If Hezekiah had any hope of recovering, it was extinguished by the word of the Lord through the prophet Isaiah. He was told to set his house in order because he was surely going to die and not live. However discouraging those words must have been, Hezekiah did what he knew, and that was to cry out! He turned his face to the wall and prayed to God who can turn any situation around. He reminded God of his life.

*Isaiah 38:3* - And said, Remember now, O Lord, I beseech thee, how I have walked before thee in truth and with a perfect heart, and have done that which is good in thy sight. And Hezekiah wept sore.

God heard Hezekiah's prayer and sent Isaiah to let him know his words had been heard and his tears had been seen. God graciously added fifteen years to his life.

We all must live with the fact that we are not going to be on this earth forever. How we use our time is extremely important. The clock is ticking this very moment. The older we get the louder the tick becomes, so we do not have any time to waste.

*Psalm 90:12* says, So teach us to number our days, that we may apply our hearts unto wisdom.

Wisdom will tell us to use our time wisely. Time is one of our most precious commodities that we cannot get back. A minute lost is a minute lost.

We must make every day count. Many people have spent years bogged down in anger and unforgiveness. Parents haven't spoken to their children, children haven't spoken to their parents, siblings shut down and refuse to speak, couples live in the same home and yet they are divided. While emotions are running amok, time is constantly moving and precious moments, hours, days, weeks, months and years are being lost. Oftentimes we give so much energy to negative emotions and things that don't matter, that our quality of life ends up being less than God prepared for us. God wants us to live abundant, fruitful lives.

According to Psalm 90:10 we have been promised seventy years, and possibly eighty if our bodies have the strength. The question of the day is, "What are you doing with this gift of time and life God has given you?" If you are reading this, you still have time. You still have time to write that book, have that seminar, start that business, call that loved one you haven't spoken to, even if they are not receptive, just make sure there are no ill feelings in your heart. Honor God by using the time he gave you wisely.

We can use our time wisely by sensitizing our ears to God's voice and asking him to order our steps. Yes, God does speak! Do you remember when you could've had an accident, and "something" told you to go another way? Well, that "something" was the voice of God. The steps of a good man (that includes women also) are ordered by the Lord. (Psalm 37:23) When we allow God to order our steps, we will definitely maximize our time. I remember when I first prayed the prayer for God to lead me and believe me, he did. I found myself being busy, busy, busy! Every time I laid down I would think of several things I didn't do before going to bed. I did not want to get up, but I did, because I knew God was aiding me in not leaving anything undone. God was delivering me from procrastination or wasting time. After many nights of having to get up and do something I'd put off, I got wise and started doing everything I needed to do before I laid down. I got tired of getting perfectly positioned on my pillow, with my comforter snuggled up around my neck then being reminded of something I should've done that day but didn't. My obedience to God brought a great awareness to me of how much time I was wasting and how many things were going undone in my life. I started making valuable changes and making every minute count. When my days on earth are up, I want to say what Jesus said, "It is finished." (St. John 19:30) Jesus was saying he'd done all he was put on this earth to do. Also, Apostle Paul said, "I have finished my course, I have kept the faith...." (II Timothy 4:7) In essence he was saying, "I didn't waste my time here on earth. I did all I was supposed to do!" Isn't that an awesome epitaph! We must remember later isn't promised to us, and the present is a gift which we should appreciate by maximizing every moment.

We can also use our time wisely by valuing today. Think about all the time and days you've wasted. Have you ever looked back over your life and wondered where all the time went? It went to whatever you were committed to. What we are committed to we put our time into. Some people are committed to working, and that's where the majority of their time, energy and effort goes, even if their family is being neglected. In the end maybe they have more money but at the price of a broken family. That is a great price to pay! We must realize that our lives today reflect how we used days in times past. How much more could we have accomplished had we not been oblivious to the hands of the clock as they moved forward? We value today by being intentional about every moment of our lives. Being intentional requires thought, organization, and follow through. Think about what you'd like to accomplish and what God's will is for your life. What has God placed on your heart to do? After thinking about it, write it down.

*Habakkuk 2:2* - And the Lord answered me and said, Write the vision, and make it plain upon tables, that he may run that readeth it.

Writing your dreams and visions down helps you to see what you'd like to accomplish. After writing down what you'd like to do, next comes the objectives. Objectives are how we plan to make our vision come to fruition. After the objectives have been clearly defined, now it is time to get to work. This is a good method to help us value each day. Each day will bring with it its own sense of accomplishments. Lord, teach us to number our days. Thank you for the gifts of life and time. Help us to use them wisely, allowing our lights to so shine before men that they may see our good works and glorify you.

Another way to value today is not to allow yesterday rob you of today. So many people live in the past. They constantly meditate on who lied on them, who stole from them, or who hurt them. I have spoken to many people who are stuck in yesterday, missing out on the beauty of today. Apostle Paul who had gone through many trials, shared a very good point with the church of Philippi:

*Philippians 3: 13-14* - Brethren, I count not myself to have apprehended: but this one thing I do, forgetting those things which are behind, and reaching forth unto those things which are before, I press toward the mark for the prize of the high calling of God in Christ Jesus.

Through the help of God there is healing for things that transpired in our past. He is a broken heart mender and he came to set the captive free. Don't be a bound captive of yesterday when God has already set you free.

Make a commitment not to waste another valuable minute. Purposefully use every day wisely. Don't live haphazardly, live intentionally! As long as there is breath in your body, you have been given the gift of time. Don't abuse it, use it. Each day you wake up ask God to order your steps and watch your level of productivity increase. Remember the story of the lady in the hospital and refuse to allow that to be you.

# Prophetic Word

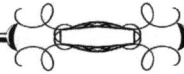

Thus saith the Lord, Use your time wisely! Do not take my words lightly, for your time on earth is a precious gift but it is limited, so value it. Do not squander it, for you do not know what tomorrow holds. Do what you can while you can, saith God. Do not allow slothfulness, fear or distractions keep you from doing what you need to do. Live not chained to hurt, anger, bitterness and unforgiveness, for these are emotions of yesterday that rob you of today. Move forward, saith the Lord. Seek me daily and allow me to order your steps so you can finish your course with joy and not regret.

# Power Scriptures

**Proverbs 27:1**
Boast not thyself of tomorrow; for thou knowest not what a day may bring forth.

**Psalm 37:1**
Commit thy way unto the Lord; trust also in him; and he shall bring it to pass.

**Psalm 37:23**
The steps of a good man are ordered by the Lord: and he delighteth in his way.

**Matthew 24:42**
Watch therefore: for ye know not what hour your Lord doth come.

**II Corinthians 6:1-2**
We then, as workers together with him, beseech you also that ye receive not the grace of God in vain. For he saith, I have heard thee in a time accepted, and in the day of salvation have I succoured thee: behold, now is the accepted time, behold, now is the day of salvation.

## Ephesians 4:26
Be ye angry and sin not: let not the sun go down upon your wrath.

## Ecclesiastes 7:14
In the day of prosperity be joyful, but in the day of adversity consider: God also hath set the one over against the other, to the end that man should find nothing after him.

## John 9:4
I must work the works of him who sent me while it is day: the night cometh, when no man can work.

# Reflections/Notes

_____
_____
_____
_____
_____
_____
_____
_____
_____
_____
_____
_____
_____
_____
_____
_____
_____
_____
_____
_____
_____
_____
_____
_____
_____

# CHAPTER SEVEN

# Too Busy to Rest

Many of us are just too busy to rest. We've got to get this done, we've got to get that done, and rest isn't anywhere on our agendas. We find ourselves pushing from one event to the next taking no time to smell the roses. Many times we don't connect with the people in our midst because we are just too busy. Nowadays since we have all types of electronics, we can literally work twenty-four hours a day, seven days a week. I heard a very ambitious person say, "I don't have time to rest or sleep. I can sleep when I am dead." The next news I received was regarding their hospitalization due to exhaustion, something that could have been avoided. Success means nothing if your body breaks down while you are achieving it. Know when to work but know when to rest. Let's take a cue from God himself.

After six days when God completed creation, he RESTED.

*Genesis 2:1-3* - Thus the heavens and the earth were finished, and all the host of them. And on the seventh day God ended his work which he had made; and rested on the seventh day from all his work which he had made. And God blessed the seventh day and sanctified it: because that in it he had rested from all his work which God created and made.

If God rested don't you think we should as well? Truly what we are doing isn't as important as what God did. God always gives us examples to follow, and in Genesis chapter 2, he rested after his labor. If God rested after he labored, why should we work ourselves to a frazzle? When we work excessively without resting, we are breaking a pattern that God set. We will talk more about that in a moment. God spoke numerous times in his Word about rest, yet we still seem to minimize its importance.

When I was a child, I remember businesses being closed on Sundays. If there was something needed for Sunday it had to be purchased Saturday. On Saturday the fragrance of pot roast, beans, greens and cornbread would fill the house as grandmother prepared Sunday's meal. Our salivary glands began working overtime in anticipation of our next day's dinner which we would eat together as a family after attending church. We would eat, rest and talk about the goodness of the Lord. Life seemed to be much less stressful and hectic during those days.

The book of Exodus also instructs us to rest. Let's look at what it says.

*Exodus 20:9-10* - Six days thou shalt labor and do all thy work. But the seventh day is the sabbath of the Lord thy God: in it thou shalt not do any work, thou, nor thy son, nor thy daughter, thy manservant, nor thy maidservant, nor thy cattle, nor thy stranger that is within thy gates.

In Genesis we are told what God did. In Exodus, not only are we told *what* God did, but *what* he wants us to do. God wants us to labor, then rest! You mean rest is a commandment? Yes, it is! We often focus on the other commandments like, do not steal, do not commit adultery, but we overlook the fact that we have been *commanded* to rest. As a society we are getting busier and busier but that is the plan of man, not the plan of God. People are working themselves into a frenzy and receiving only what they can get for themselves. When we follow God's plan he works on our behalf and the benefits we receive are far greater.

So, the question is, when was the last time you rested? No, I mean really rested! When was the last time you took time to smell the roses? When was the last time you spent a day with God? When was the last time you didn't let your telephone or other electronic devices rule you? Can't remember? Well, maybe it's time! It is time for us to stop overextending ourselves until our bodies are exhausted, depleted, and our immune system breaks down. Sickness then forces us to do what we should have done in the first place, and that is to stop and rest. If this is you, don't run to the prayer line for prayer, "Repent" and get some rest!

Now, back to Genesis. After six days of intense working, God rested on the seventh day. Did God rest because he was tired? No, he was trying to show us the importance of balance. Too much work or too much rest causes our lives to be off balance. Too much of anything is out of balance. God hates a false balance according to Proverbs.

*Proverbs 11:1* A false balance is an abomination to the Lord: but a just weight is his delight.

We must live a life of balance and not allow work or anything else to consume our lives. When we do not rest something has become an idol in our lives. God said he will have no other gods before him. (Selah – pause and think about that). We are made in the image of God, so let's mirror his image by making time to rest. We must be intentional about resting. When we rest we are showing God we are trusting and depending upon him. We all need time to just breathe! Many ministry leaders are guilty of breaking this biblical principle of rest. We must do what we can and trust God for the rest. We must remember, we are not God, but tools of God. We are all a spirit, we have a soul and live in a *body*, so rest is important for our well-being. If you are one who focuses on being obedient to God, well, resting is part of that obedience and it is his will! Do not feel guilty for getting necessary rest.

Not only do we need natural, (physical) rest, but our soul, which consists of our mind, will, and emotions, needs rest as well. As important as each of these are, they are often neglected in our lives. We cannot rest our souls if we do not trust God. The two go hand in hand. Our minds work overtime trying to find solutions to the problems we face when we don't trust God. In I Peter the Bible clearly tells us what to do.

*I Peter 5:7* Casting all your care upon him; for he careth for you.

The word cast, according to the Oxford Dictionary, means to throw something forcefully in a specified direction. God is telling us not to worry, stress or strain, but throw all our woes to him because he omnipotent, which means all powerful. He can handle anything. Oftentimes we cannot rest because we haven't yielded our problems to God. Casting our cares and resting requires faith: faith in the Word of God, and faith in the God of the Word. Faith requires a release that says, "Lord, I know you've got this!" I like to say, "Our *"knowers"* must be working." When our *knowers* are working we find a Scripture that states what God has done concerning our situation; we read it, study it, proclaim it, pray it and patiently wait on God. Impatient waiting is not resting, it is wrestling! When we are resting, we have surrendered the situation to God and are listening for his solution. When we are trying to find our own solutions, we are wrestling. Numerous times in my life when it seemed like God was ignoring me, I would begin to devise and carry out my own plan. The next thing I heard was, "Boom!" Yes, my plan that seemed to be so perfect did not work! God knows what is best for us and we should wait patiently for him to work on our behalf. I have since learned to stop wasting time with my own plan because God's plan always trumps mine! God is so gracious. He led me to the following Scriptures and now they are a great part of my life: Jeremiah 10:23 and Proverbs 16:9.

*Jeremiah 10:23* - O Lord, I know that the way of man is not in himself: it is not in man that walketh to direct his steps.

*Proverbs 16:9* – A man's heart deviseth his way: but the Lord directeth his steps.

Bearing those Scriptures in mind you must ask yourself, "Am I resting or wrestling?" Be honest with yourself because you know!

The Bible gives us explicit directions about how to achieve rest for our souls. We must **labor** to enter into rest. Needless to say, we don't enter into rest until we have labored. How do we rest and labor at the same time? It's an oxymoron, but not impossible. Let's look at Hebrews chapter 4:

Hebrews 4:10-11 - For he that is entered into his rest, he also hath ceased from his own works, as God did from his.

Let us therefore labor to enter into that rest...

We enter into rest when we stop doing what we want to do, or what we think we should do, and do what we NEED to DO! The work we need to do is to implement the Word of God in our lives. Sometimes while we are implementing the Word, the desired results seem slow to manifest which is where the work comes in. Actually, the work is in keeping the faith while waiting. Keep doing the Word! Keep doing the Word! Keep doing the Word! How long do we do the Word? We do the Word until we see the manifestation of the promise fulfilled in our lives. No stressing, no wrestling, just resting in God and his promises. He is a promise keeper and he is not going to use us for his promise breaking project!

Rest in the fact that Father God has already provided everything we need. We don't have to get in the daily grind so hard that we neglect caring for our bodies and wear our souls down to a frazzle. Let's honor God by trusting him and knowing he is omnipotent, which is all powerful, omniscient, all knowing, and omnipresent, everywhere at the same time. God cares for you, so REST. Don't worry. REST! Don't stress. REST!

Don't work yourself to death! REST!

# Prophetic Word

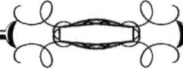

Thus saith the Lord, you are my workmanship. I made you in my image and after my likeness. I gave you power, dominion and authority. I made you with a drive to succeed, but do not abuse and neglect your body in the process. Although I fashioned you like me, saith God, I am a Spirit. I do not have a body and I am not governed by physical laws, but your body needs rest. It needs rest to restore, repair and replenish itself. I have given you a pattern in my Word. Follow the pattern, saith God. Following the pattern keeps the door closed to the enemy. When you do not follow the pattern, you are telling the enemy he has open access to come in and wreak havoc not only in your body but also in your life. Rest, rest, rest, saith the Lord! Do not be a lawbreaker, saith God. Follow my laws! Follow my precepts! Follow my statutes and you will find yourself more productive than ever before. Trust me, saith the Lord, for I am the ultimate provider!

# Power Scriptures

### Psalm 3:5
I laid me down and slept; I awaked; for the Lord sustained me.

### Psalm 127:2
It is vain for you to rise up early, to sit up late, to eat the bread of sorrows: for so he giveth his beloved sweet sleep.

### Matthew 11:28-30
Come unto me, all ye that labor and are heavy laden, and I will give you rest. Take my yoke upon you, and learn of me; for I am meek and lowly in heart: and ye shall find rest for your souls. For my yoke is easy and my burden is light.

### Mark 6:30-32
And the apostles gathered themselves together unto Jesus, and told him all things, both what they had done, and what they taught. And he said unto them, Come ye yourselves apart into a desert place, and rest a while: for there were many coming and going, and they had no leisure so much as to eat. And they departed into a desert place by ship privately.

## Psalm 37:7

Rest in the Lord, and wait patiently for him: fret not thyself because of him who prospereth in his way, because of the man who bringeth wicked devices to pass.

## Psalm 4:8

I will both lay me down in peace, and sleep: for thou, Lord, only makest me to dwell in safety.

## Hebrews 4:9-10

There remaineth therefore a rest to the people of God. Let us therefore labour to enter into that rest.

# Reflections/Notes

# CHAPTER EIGHT

# My Body, His Temple

There have been numerous times in my life when I've gone on a health journey. I would go to the fitness center and work out, sometimes for two hours. I would also take vitamins and supplements trying to make sure I was healthy as possible. After a while my routine was broken and I could not seem to get back on track. Every day I was going to start exercising and taking care of my body tomorrow. I am ashamed to say how many tomorrows passed as I continued making excuses. Am I the only one who has made excuses? Excuses get us nowhere; it is time to become disciplined. People often change when tragedy strikes, but why not change to avoid tragedy? The time for change is NOW! We can make the necessary changes through the power of the Holy Spirit, the very presence of God who resides on our inside.

*I Corinthians 6:19–20* - Know ye not that your body is the temple of the Holy Ghost which is in you, which ye have of God, and ye are not your own? For ye are bought with a price: therefore glorify God in your body, and your spirit, which are God's.

In this chapter Apostle Paul is addressing the church and letting them know that sexual immorality defiles the body. He shares with them how to honor God by not disrespecting their bodies because their bodies house the Spirit of God. We must respect our bodies by being careful what we do and also what we put in them. At one time my husband and I owned a Jaguar S-Type, a very beautiful luxury car. This particular vehicle called for premium gasoline only. During that time premium gasoline had risen to almost $4.00 a gallon. No matter how we wanted to save money, never once did we fill the tank with regular unleaded because we knew it would cause dire consequences. We followed the manufacturer's instructions. If we could be that conscientious in taking care of our vehicles, how much more emphasis should we put on taking care of our bodies? What we value we take care of. Sometimes we value things more than our own health, or even people for that matter, but that is another subject. Since our body is the temple that houses the Spirit of God, it should be honored at all times.

In the body of Christ we address many issues in the church: adultery, fornication, lying, unforgiveness, and the list goes on and on. Two issues rarely addressed are GLUTTONY and TEMPERANCE! Occasionally we hear about temperance regarding our attitudes, but not our appetites. Gluttony causes us to eat when we aren't hungry, and also what we don't need. Usually what our bodies crave are things that are detrimental rather than beneficial to our health. Why? It's that fleshly nature that is still running wild. Rather than getting our souls healed and delivered we try to comfort our flesh by eating, or indulging in other vices, which is like putting a band aid on a shark bite. Sounds ridiculous doesn't it? It sounds ridiculous because it is! The belly may be full, but the wound or void is still there. Nothing is more comforting or healing than the Word of God. When our eating, or anything else in our life seems to be getting out of control we must push away the plate and follow Jesus' example. This is how Jesus handled Satan when he came to him with temptation.

*Luke 4:3* - And the devil said unto him, If thou be the Son of God, command this stone that it be made bread.

Jesus did not yield to the temptation. He was not confused about being the Son of God, and neither was he going to take orders from the devil. Jesus boldly spoke the Word to him.

*Luke 4:4* - And Jesus answered him, saying, It is written, That man shall not live by bread alone, but by every word that proceedeth out of the mouth of God.

Jesus was able to say, "It is written," because he knew what was written. In Luke 4, Jesus is quoting from Deuteronomy 8:3. How did he know what was written? He knew because he was a student of the Word. He didn't have Google, or anyone around for him to ask. The Word had to be *alive* in him. The Word must be alive in us as well! As followers of Christ we must develop an appetite for the Word that is greater than the appetite we have for food or anything else. We must tame our natural appetite by a word many don't like to hear, so I will say it over and over again, FASTING, FASTING, FASTING! Jesus, the most spiritual man who ever lived, *fasted*. If Jesus pulled away from food how much more should we? When food controls us, it has become our god! Sometimes we are more obedient to our stomachs than we are to God! That may be a slap in the face, but it is reality. Philippians chapter three talks about some believers who had started walking contrary to the gospel. Apostle Paul called them enemies of the cross and said their stomach [appetite] had become their god.

*Philippians 3:18-19* - For, as I have often told you before and now tell you again with tears, many live as enemies of the cross of Christ. Their destiny is destruction, their god is their stomach, and their glory is in their shame. Their mind is set on earthly things. (NIV)

The Scripture notes that their stomach, appetite, or their *flesh*, had become their god. We must be careful not to allow this to happen to us! Have you ever been sitting around your house and thought about something you'd like to eat that you didn't have? Before you knew it, you were in the car driving to the grocery store, purchasing something to eat that you didn't need. Wouldn't it be awesome if we moved like that when God wakes us up in the middle of the night and tells us to pray? He wants us to be more obedient to him than we are to our stomachs, or our flesh.

God wants us to take care of our bodies, but not only that, we should want to take care of them. Father has promised us seventy years, and eighty if we are strong, so why not live them as healthy as possible.

*Psalm 90:10* - The days of our years are threescore years and ten; and if by reason of strength they be fourscore years...

We have been promised a certain amount of time here on earth and our bodies will go through the natural aging process. We do not have to be broken down with sicknesses brought on by lack of proper care for ourselves. A Scripture that encourages me as I age is found in the following passage:

*Psalm 92:13-14* - Those that be planted in the house of the Lord shall flourish in the courts of our God. They shall still bring forth fruit in their old age; they shall be fat and flourishing.

Those are promises I am looking forward to. I am planted in God's house and I expect to flourish and bring forth fruit as I age. I have already begun making changes with great expectation. I started a health group named, My Body His Temple. It is designed to bring people into an awareness of the benefits of proper eating, and the detriment of improper eating. The importance of physical exercise is stressed as well.

About ten years ago I was diagnosed with hypertension and was prescribed medication. Many times I stopped taking my medication but without making the necessary dietary changes. Needless to say, I had to start taking it again. I am not suggesting anyone should stop taking their meds. This is a decision I made. Please check with your physician first. I refuse to be on medication for the rest of my life, so for the past months I have implemented numerous changes. Periodically I have faltered, but I do not allow that to discourage me. I just repent and move forward. I pray someone is encouraged and motivated to make changes as well. Listed below are some of the changes I have made.

1. Decrease in fried foods
2. No pork
3. Low sodium intake
4. Small intake of anything prepackaged
5. Increased water intake
6. Low caffeine intake
7. Eating more vegetables (even ones I have never liked)
8. Exercising several times per week
9. Proper rest
10. Minimal sweets

Those are some of the natural changes I have made along with prayer and fasting. I have reaped many benefits, some of which are: better working digestive system, clearer skin, clearer eyes, slight weight loss and more energy. I am still working on the hypertension, but I am sure I will have a victorious testimony in the near future. Thank God for the results I have received thus far. There are great health benefits prepared for you, but you must be willing to do the WORK! I encourage each of you to start making changes if you have not already done so. Great results are awaiting you. Remember, you will not be working alone; the Holy Spirit, who is our helper, will assist you all the way. Don't keep him waiting!

# Prophetic Word

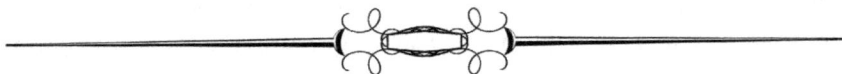

Thus saith the Lord, You are specially crafted by me. I am your Creator and I made you for my purpose. Your body is the place I have chosen to reside. You are carriers of my presence. Glorify me in your bodies. Honor me with your bodies. As you begin to have natural cravings, feed yourselves with the spiritual food of my Word. Begin to crave more of me, more of my presence; spend quality time with me and you will see great manifestations in your life. Have you not been crying out for miracles, signs and wonders, saith God? I desire to manifest them in your life, but I am waiting to see a hunger for me greater than you have for natural food. Hear me when I tell you to push away the plate. Do not turn a deaf ear. Many health issues in the lives of my people could have been avoided by hearing and obeying my voice. Hear me now. Obey me now and I will turn things around in your health. I will turn things around in your life. Did not I speak through the prophet Isaiah explaining the benefits of fasting? Many are trying to eat their burdens away, but my remedy is to fast. Many are dealing with health issues that could have been avoided, but through fasting I will cause your health to spring forth speedily, saith God. Through fasting, things the enemy have been trying to yoke you up with will be broken. Trust me, saith God. Lean on me, saith God. If you are ready for change, change is ready for you. Healing and deliverance awaits you. Do not be a hindrance to yourself. Kingdom assignments are waiting for you. Your body is my temple and I am ready to manifest myself through you in a greater way than ever before. I am calling you to a higher place in the Spirit, and a healthier place in the natural. Follow my leading. I will not lead you wrong, saith the Lord God Almighty.

# Power Scriptures

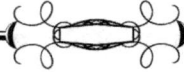

### I Corinthians 6:19-20
What? Know ye not that your body is the temple of the Holy Ghost which is in you, which ye have of God, and ye are not your own? For ye are bought with a price: therefore glorify God in your body, and in your spirit which are God's.

### Jeremiah 15:16
Thy words were found, and I did eat them; and thy word was unto me the joy and rejoicing of my heart: for I am called by thy name, O Lord God of hosts.

### Romans 12:1-2
I beseech you therefore, brethren, by the mercies of God, that ye present your bodies a living sacrifice, holy, acceptable unto God, which is your reasonable service. And be not conformed to this world: but be ye transformed by the renewing of your mind, that ye may prove what is that good, and acceptable, and perfect will of God.

### I Corinthians 9:27
But I keep under my body, and bring it unto subjection: lest by any means, when I have preached to others, I myself should be a castaway.

### I Corinthians 3:16-17
Know ye not that ye are the temple of God, and that the Spirit of God dwelleth in you. If any man defile the temple of God, him shall God destroy, for the temple of God is holy, which temple ye are.

### Job 23:12
Neither have I gone back from the commandment of his lips; I have esteemed the words of his mouth more than my necessary food.

### Romans 1:22-24
Professing themselves to be wise, they became fools, And changed the glory of the uncorruptible God into an image made like to corruptible man, and to birds, and fourfooted beasts, and creeping things. Wherefore God also gave them over to uncleanness through the lusts of their own heart, to dishonor their own bodies between themselves: Who changed the truth of God into a lie, and worshipped and served the creature more than the Creator, who is blessed forever. Amen.

### Psalm 100:3
Know ye that the Lord he is God: it is he that hath made us, and not we ourselves; we are his people, and the sheep of his pasture.

### Proverbs 17:22
A merry heart doeth good like a medicine: but a broken spirit drieth the bones.

# Reflections/Notes

_____
_____
_____
_____
_____
_____
_____
_____
_____
_____
_____
_____
_____
_____
_____
_____
_____
_____
_____
_____
_____
_____
_____
_____
_____
_____

——————

# CHAPTER NINE

# Live Fully While You Are Living

L ife gives you one shot! Make the best of it! The quality of your life depends on you. You must take responsibility for YOU! Many people live their lives waiting on someone else to make them happy, fill voids in their soul, or cater to their brokenness rather than get healed. If you are unhappy with your life **you** can turn things around starting today.

For many years I lived as a victim, but I didn't know it. I thought that was just me. Thank God, one day I found out that wasn't me. I'd allowed situations and circumstances in my life to mold me into a sad, sorrowful and non-confident individual. No longer was I that bright-eyed little girl who thought she could do anything, even run faster than boys and climb trees better than them! Lol! I have three brothers and no sisters, so I was pretty tough. Somewhere along the line after being physically, verbally and emotionally abused, I became who life made me. I lived many years in anger and bitterness. I was walled up and not enjoying life. I spent many days just existing, but with a smile on my face trying to hide my pain. One day I was looking at a television show and I heard these words, "pivotal moments." The word "pivotal" according to Webster means "very important" or "critical." "Moment" means "a precise point in time." The person said the choices you make in these moments can take you up or cause you to spiral downward. It was in that moment that I realized I'd been making choices that diminished my power, thus causing me to live as a victim rather than a victor. I immediately began evaluating my life and finding out where I'd lost myself. I began a journey of spending quality time with God, and as he revealed certain things, I would release them to him. He was always ready, willing, and able to receive everything I laid on him. The more time I spent with Father, the more freedom I received in my soul. The real me began to emerge and it felt good! I have maintained my freedom by finding Scriptures that related to whatever I may have been dealing with and applying them in my life. Freedom is having faith in the Word of God above all else. A perfect description of God's Word is found in the following verse:

*Hebrews 4:12* - The word of God is quick, and powerful, and sharper than a twoedged sword, piercing even to the dividing asunder of soul and spirit, and of the joints and marrow, and is a discerner of the thoughts and intents of the heart.

When we become doers of God's Word we receive the benefit of it cutting through any negativity we may be faced with. God has an awesome plan for our lives; it is for us to live victoriously and walk in dominion on a daily basis. We must "*know*" this or we will find ourselves wasting precious valuable time that Father has blessed us with. Don't neglect the blessing of time. There is a lady in the Bible in I Samuel who lived many years of her life in sorrow because she was barren. I am definitely not minimizing her situation, but sadness couldn't change it. Her husband Elkanah also had another wife named Peninnah who was having baby after baby. If that wasn't enough, Peninnah taunted Hannah daily. Hannah was vexed, depressed, and cried for years. Sometimes she was so depressed she couldn't eat. According to their custom, she and her family would go to the temple yearly to sacrifice and worship. For years Hannah would go to the temple depressed and come home depressed. Time was constantly passing and she was missing out on the beauty of life she could've been experiencing. She allowed what she didn't have, and someone else's negative behavior to rule her life. She had given her power away. Be careful not to allow this to be you! One year as they were preparing to go to the temple, Hannah must have had an epiphany, an aha moment, because this time when she arrived at the temple she cried but the tears were different. She cried before God and to him. Finally, she cast her care on the one who was able to make a difference!

The Bible says in I Samuel 1:10 – 11:
And she was in bitterness of soul, and she prayed unto the Lord and wept sore. And she vowed a vow, and said, O Lord of hosts, if thou wilt indeed look on the affliction of thine handmaid, and remember me, and not forget thine handmaid, but will give unto thine handmaid a man child, then I will give him unto the Lord all the days of his life, and there shall no razor come upon his head.

This was Hannah's pivotal moment. She could have gone to the temple and done the same thing she had done the previous years, but this time she made up her mind to do something different. She decided to give God her prayer request and surrender every ill feeling to him. She prayed so hard that the priest Eli thought she was drunk. She poured her soul out to the Lord! She made up in her mind that she was no longer going to be a burden carrier. No longer was she going to be vexed and depressed. She decided to be free! Freedom is a choice and thank God she chose it. You can choose it too! When she *"freed herself"* through prayer, Eli told her to go in peace, and that her petition had been granted! Upon leaving the temple, Hannah's appetite was restored and sadness was no longer a part of her life. She left the temple a new woman! Hallelujah!

*I Samuel 1:18* - So the woman went her way, and did eat, and her countenance was no more sad.

The story goes on to say that the next day they got up early and **worshiped** before the Lord. Hannah is no longer crying, but she is worshiping. There is victory in worship! There is healing in worship! There is deliverance in worship! Worship is what God wanted from Hannah all along. Worship, which is spiritual intimacy, is what God wants from us as well. He wants us to lose ourselves in him through worship. Because Hannah lost herself in intimacy with God, the next time she was intimate with her husband her womb was opened, she conceived and bare a son. Not only did she have a son, he became a priest and a judge in Israel. Isn't that awesome!

The same freedom God gave myself and Hannah can be yours as well. No longer do you have to live as a victim. Don't waste another precious moment. Don't let life take the life out of you! Take your life back! Decide today not to allow anything you have gone through steal from you any longer. Take authority over what has been taking authority over you by casting every care on the Lord because he cares for you.

Purpose to implement God's Word in every situation that occurs in your life. God has a beautiful life planned for you and it is time for you to live it.

*Jeremiah 29:11-14* - For I know the thoughts that I think toward you, saith the Lord, thoughts of peace and not of evil, to give you an expected end. Then shall ye call upon me, and ye shall go, and pray unto me, and I will hearken unto you. And ye shall seek me, and find me, when ye shall search for me with all your heart. And I will be found of you, saith the Lord: and I will turn your captivity.

God has an awesome plan for your life. He is thinking peaceful thoughts about you so why should you think otherwise? It doesn't matter what anyone else is thinking. What God thinks trumps everything! Father has a hope and a future planned for you. (Amplified Bible). You can enter into this goodness by calling on God, praying to him, seeking him, and searching for him with all your heart. He promises to be found of you and that he would turn your captivity. He does not break his promises, and neither does he lie.

*II Corinthians 1:20* - For all the promises of God in him are yea, and in him Amen, unto the glory of God by us.

*Numbers 23:19* - God is not a man that he should lie; neither the son of man that he should repent: hath he said, and shall he not do it? or hath he spoken, and shall he not make it good?

God will fulfill every promise he has made. When you do your part, he will definitely do his! Everything that has had you bound has to release you, and you can begin to live and not simply exist!

Live fully while you are living! Live! Live! Live!

# Prophetic Word

Thus saith the Lord, Do not let what you go through cause you to miss out on life. You do not have to carry old hurts and wounds, but give them to me, saith God. I sent my Son to bind up the brokenhearted and to set the captives free. Why should you live a life of bondage when I have set freedom before you? Don't lose any more time in the clutches of the wounds of yesterday, but live in my promises today. My Son received stripes on his back for you, not only for your physical healing, but healing for every area of your life. Receive your healing, saith the Lord, and LIVE! I desire for you to live and not just exist. I desire for you to have life and life more abundantly, not just having a bunch of things, but walking in complete healing and deliverance. I am a soul restorer, saith God. I am here for you. Seek me like never before. Pour your heart out to me. Don't get lost in those who did you wrong, but get lost in me, the one who holds the key to your deliverance. Receive your deliverance, LIVE and not just exist, saith the Lord thy God!

# Power Scriptures

**Psalm 16:11**
Thou wilt shew me the path of life: in thy presence is fulness of joy; at thy right hand there are pleasures evermore.

**James 4:14**
Whereas ye know not what shall be on the morrow. For what is your life? It is even a vapour, that now appeareth for a little time, and then vanisheth away.

**Colossians 3:23**
...whatsoever ye do, do it heartily, as to the Lord, and not unto men.

**Psalm 146:2**
While I live will I praise the Lord: I will sing praises unto my God while I have any being.

**II Corinthians 5:17**
Therefore, if any man be in Christ, he is a new creature: old things are passed away: behold, all things are become new.

**Psalm 23:1**
The Lord is my shepherd; I shall not want.

## Romans 8:28

And we know that all things work together for good to them that love God, to them who are the called according to his purpose.

## Proverbs 3:5-6

Trust in the Lord with all thine heart; and lean not unto thine own understanding. In all thy ways acknowledge him, and he shall direct thy paths.

# Reflections/Notes

CHAPTER TEN

# Don't Eat the Devil's Food

Don't eat the devil's food! What kind of topic is that? Well, I am so glad you asked. As you read a little further you may find you've been guilty of doing just that. When we eat the devil's food we get the fruit of mayhem, disgust, disappointment, sadness, anger and a plethora of negative emotions and manifestations. Satan is crafty and cunning, but we do not have to be taken by his craftiness. "Do not" are the operative words in the previous statement. We must recognize when the devil is serving his dish and refuse to accept it. Would you accept a beautifully garnished silver platter of cow manure served by one of the top chefs in America? I'm inclined to believe you wouldn't. Just as you would reject that platter of ridiculousness, reject everything the devil tries to serve.

I am reminded of one of my childhood stories my family shares every time we get together. We laugh as though it is the first time we have ever heard it. Not only do we laugh, but we laugh until tears roll down our faces, because we don't just tell the story, we act it out as well. Every summer my younger brother and I would be sent to the country to stay with our great grandparents. We did not have a lot of toys or other children to play with, so we had to use our imagination. Since I was six years older than him my imagination was a little more vivid. It was a beautiful sunny but partly cloudy day. As I looked at the horizon the clouds looked as if they were touching the earth. Since I had nothing else to do but harass my little brother, I couldn't allow this opportunity to pass me by. I told my brother to look at the sky and I began to frantically say, "The sky is falling!" I was trying to make him panic, but he did not budge. He stood flat-footed, clenched his fist with his arms to his side, eyes bulging, the vein in his neck protruding, and said with all his might, "No, that sky ain't fallinnnnn!!!!!" No matter how I tried to feed him an untruth, he refused to accept it. He was about four years old at the time, but he was tenacious and unwavering in the truth he knew! Thank God he didn't believe the nonsense I was telling him. He refused to eat what was being served. He could've accepted it, but he refused. He made a choice; a right choice. Question – what choice do you make when a platter of negativity and ridiculousness is being served? You have the power to make the right choice!

There is a character in the Bible named Samson, whose life had a tragic end because he ate what the devil served, even though he knew better. When you know better you are supposed to do better, but that is not always the case, as it was for Samson. He allowed his emotions to get the best of him. He totally neglected his relationship with God for a lustful, fleshly relationship. He was somewhere, with someone he shouldn't have been with, doing something he shouldn't have been doing. He was setting himself up for failure.

Samson fell in love with a Philistine whore named Delilah. According to Dictionary.net, Delilah means temptress. She used her feminine wiles to get Samson to fall in love with her. Although he was in love with her, she was not in love with him. This relationship was out of balance in many ways. Samson did not heed any of the signs; he ate everything Delilah served. We must not want a relationship so badly that we close our eyes to all the flags that are being presented. (This is for all of you who are dating) When you are dating there are some things you just DO NOT have to put up with! Know when to call it QUITS!

Now, back to Samson. Samson was born to a woman who had been barren. One day she had a visitation from the angel of the Lord who gave her this awesome message:

*Judges 13:3-5* - ...Behold now, thou art barren, and bearest not: but thou shalt conceive and bear a son. Now therefore beware, I pray thee, and drink not wine nor strong drink, and eat not any unclean thing. For lo, thou shalt conceive, and bear a son; and no razor shall come on his head: for the child shall be a Nazarite unto God from the womb: and he shall begin to deliver Israel out of the hand of the Philistines.

Samson was a special child whose purpose was noted before his birth. He was called to be a Nazarite from his mother's womb which meant he belonged to God and had certain restrictions on his life. As long as Samson followed those restrictions he remained in covenant with God and was a possessor of supernatural strength. The Philistines hated Samson because he had defeated them on numerous occasions. They were determined to find out where his strength came from. When they found out he was involved with Delilah, one of their own, they saw an opportunity to get the information they wanted. The lords of the Philistines came to Delilah and offered her eleven hundred pieces of silver per person to entice Samson to tell her where he got his strength. Well, they came up with a perfect plan, because Samson loved Delilah. Unfortunately for him, Delilah's feelings were not the same. Delilah loved money! Using her feminine wiles, she pressed and pressed Samson until he could take it no more.

Finally, he ate what the devil served him in the form of a Philistine whore.

*Judges 16:15-18* - And she said unto him, How canst thou say, I love thee, when thine heart is not with me? Thou hast mocked me these three times, and hast not told me wherein thy great strength lieth. And it came to pass, when she pressed him daily with her words, and urged him, so that his soul was vexed unto death; That he told her all his heart, and said unto her, There hath not come a razor upon mine head; for I have been a Nazarite unto God from my mother's womb: if I be shaven, then my strength will go from me, and I shall be like any other man. And when Delilah saw he told her all his heart, she sent and called for the Philistines, saying, Come up this once, for he hath shewed me all his heart. Then the lords of the Philistines came up unto her, and brought money in their hand.

Just as the enemy constantly plotted against Samson, he is always plotting against you as well, trying to see how he can bring you down. He does not want to see you successful in any area of your life. He especially does not want you doing the will of God. He wants to disrupt your relationship with God and try to get you to walk contrary to his Word, thus negating the promises that belong to you. The enemy was successful in disrupting Samson's relationship with God by using Delilah. After lying to Delilah three times about his strength, eventually he conceded, ultimately eating the devil's food which led to his demise. He knew she was betraying him to the Philistines, yet he refused to end their relationship. He kept eating the devil's food. As he took a nap on Delilah's lap, the Philistines came and cut off the seven locks of his hair that hadn't been cut since birth. The Nazarite covenant had now been broken and Samson no longer possessed supernatural strength. He had to rely on his own limited ability.

At this point the Philistines bound him, gouged his eyes out and made him a slave. Eventually he would die with the Philistines. Anytime we eat the devil's food in any form we must remember there are dire consequences. He served up a platter of lust to Samson, and he ate and ate and ate. He knew just what to serve Samson and he knows what to serve you: he knows your buttons and points of weakness. That is why it is so important to allow the Word of God to bring freedom in every area of our lives so there will be no buttons, and we must present every weakness to God. In our weakness he is made strong. We must remember what Jesus did when he was in the wilderness being tempted of the devil. He refused to eat what Satan was serving! Jesus overcame Satan by saying, "It is written." If we apply "It is written" in our lives when being served a platter of nothingness from the adversary, we will always come out victoriously. We must stay vigilant and in constant submission to God, resisting the devil, causing him to flee.

Refuse to eat the devil's food!

# Prophetic Word

Thus saith the Lord, Be sober, be vigilant; because your adversary the devil, as a roaring lion, goeth about seeking whom he may devour. I have already overthrown him, saith God, and because you are my children he is constantly after you. I have given you everything you need to walk in victory. Know who you are, saith God, and the power you possess! I have given you power over all the power of the enemy, so when Satan comes your way, do not submit to him, do not yield to his tactics, but use the power I have given you and you will come out victoriously every time! Keep your spirit strong through prayer, studying, meditating and doing my Word. Let my Word have free course in you, that when the enemy comes he will find every door closed. Remember my Word, resist the devil and he will flee from you, saith the Lord thy God!

# Power Scriptures

## Matthew 26:41

Watch and pray, lest ye enter into temptation. The spirit truly is willing, but the flesh is weak.

## II Peter 2:9

The Lord knoweth how to deliver the godly out of temptations, and reserve the unjust unto the day of judgment to be punished:

## I Peter 5:8

Be sober, be vigilant; because your adversary the devil as a roaring lion, walketh about, seeking whom he may devour:

## Proverbs 6:27-28

Can a man take fire in his bosom, and his clothes not get burned? Can one go upon hot coals, and his feet not be burned?

## Hebrews 2:17-18

Wherefore in all things it behoved him to be made like unto his brethren, that he might be a merciful and faithful high priest in things pertaining to God, to make reconciliation for the sins of the people. For in that he himself hath suffered being tempted, he is able to succour them that are tempted.

## Colossians 3:1-3

If ye then be risen with Christ, seek those things which are above, where Christ is seated on the right hand of God. Set your affection on things above, not on things on the earth. For ye are dead, and your life is hid with Christ in God.

# Reflections/Notes

# CHAPTER ELEVEN

# You Can Do It Too!

Why sit on the sidelines of life and watch everyone else succeed? It's one thing to see someone else win and cheer them on, but it is more gratifying when you win and others are cheering you on. It's one thing to look at motivational videos, but how much better would it be if you made your own and let someone watch yours? You can do it! The only difference between you and them is they did it, and you didn't. It is one thing to talk about what you are going to do, but it is another thing to do it. God is not looking for talkers, he is looking for doers. In the book of Matthew, Jesus spoke a parable to some religious leaders who were always telling others what to do but were guilty of not doing it themselves. Let's take a look.

*Matthew 21:28-31* - But what think ye? A certain man

had two sons; and he came to the first, and said, Son, go work today in my vineyard. He answered and said, I will not: but afterward he repented, and went. And he came to the second, and said likewise. And he answered and said, I go, sir: and went not. Whether of the twain did the will of his father? They say unto him, The first.

After they gave Jesus the most obvious and correct answer, he went on to rebuke them because they knew what to do but weren't doing it. They were talkers and not doers. We must become doers and not just talkers!

Over the years I've attended many church services and I would be given prophetic words about writing books. With sparkles in my eyes, and a smile on my face, I would clap my hands in excitement. "God, you want me to write a book?" I began to talk about the book I was going to write. I had the title and I knew the essence of the book but could not seem to pen any of my thoughts. For years people would ask me, "Have you written your book?" My response would be, "No, not yet, but I'm going to." I really meant the words I said but I was having difficulty overcoming obstacles and hindrances. Well, eventually I became embarrassed and I did not want to see certain people because I knew what they were going to ask me. I became tired of hiding due to embarrassment; not only embarrassment, but also disobedience to God. I had to do something! On numerous occasions I was determined to write my book but every time I sat down to write I couldn't seem to come up with five good sentences.

It was extremely frustrating so I would move on to another task leaving that one unfinished. Are there things in your life that have been left undone, for whatever reason? Hmm! Just asking. What was my problem? After much cogitation I realized the problem was in my mind and not in my writing ability. No longer could I succumb to the mental block that reared its head every time I sat down to write. When I realized I had been defeating myself, the words "I can't" had to leave my mind.

*Philippians 4:13* – I can do all things through Christ which strengtheneth me.

My husband and I have a good friend, named Dr. Stan Harris, aka, Dr. Breakthrough. He is an awesome motivational speaker and has spoken all over the USA. He devised a quote that has been a tremendous blessing to me and has revolutionized my life.

His quote says: "Once I make up my mind to do something, God will orchestrate circumstances to align themselves in my favor. When I say, "I can't" my mind stops trying. But when I ask, "How?" my mind keeps searching until it finds a way. There is a way, and I will find it. If not, by the grace of God, I will invent it!"

That profound statement was the extra fuel I needed to fulfill my writing assignment. I decided as I was writing and difficulty would arise, rather than allow my mind draw a blank,

I would stop, breathe, talk to God and myself, gather a little more information, then, continue writing. No longer were mental blocks going to defeat me. I was going to get this book out of my mind and onto paper! Please know that whenever you decide to progress in life there will always be hindrances, but you must make up your mind to be an overcomer so you won't be an underachiever.

An awesome overcomer who happens to be one of my favorite Biblical characters is Nehemiah. Nehemiah was cupbearer to King Artaxerses. Although he was servant to the king, God had placed many skills and abilities inside of him. One day he was told that his fellow people, the Jews, were not doing well. The walls of Jerusalem had been torn down and the gates had been burned with fire. This brought Nehemiah to tears. He could've just cried and talked about what a bad situation that was, but he did more. He began to pray, fast and devise a plan to rebuild the wall. To keep a long story short, as he began to implement his plan, two naysayers, Sanballat and Tobiah came to him, bringing every hindrance you could imagine: ridicule, criticism, intimidation, threats, conspiracy, and many other things. Nehemiah did not let any of that stop him and his people from rebuilding the wall and setting up the gates. He overcame everything the enemy brought his way through prayer and remembering God. God gave Nehemiah strategy after strategy, and as he implemented them, he always came out victoriously. The wall was finished in fifty-two days! The city of Jerusalem was once again fortified, and the enemy could no longer go in and come out as pleased. Every enemy that had come up against Nehemiah and his constituents had to bow to the fact that their best efforts did not work.

*Nehemiah 6:15* - And it came to pass when all our enemies heard thereof, and all the enemies saw these things (the finished wall), they were much cast down in their own eyes: for they perceived that this was **the work of our God.**

Nehemiah overcame every obstacle and hindrance that came against him. He saw his vision come to fruition. His victorious life gives us a great example to follow. It is also extremely encouraging. Now, with that said, I was determined to debilitate and annihilate every barrier and hindrance that would come my way. I decided to sit down, be an open channel and write whatever flowed out of my heart via Holy Spirit! Here I am now, writing, and I am determined to continue! What changed? My mind changed because of the ammunition I was presented with; prayer, fasting, the quote from Dr. Breakthrough, and the story of Nehemiah. Like Nehemiah, I made a plan. I was going to get up each morning, open my computer and sit before it like I was at work. I knew I couldn't sit there all day doing nothing. Something had to happen, and one day it did! Thoughts started flowing and my fingers started moving over the keys on my laptop and you are seeing the fruit of it today. Thank you, Jesus!

I used to work for a lady when I was in my late teens and she would always tell me a quote from Booker T. Washington, "Plan your work, and work your plan." That is a good motto!

If you don't plan anything, your efforts will be scattered. Nothing is what you get when your efforts are scattered. STOP being COMMITTED TO NOTHING! Make a plan, commit to it, and follow through.

When I decided to treat writing like a job, I began to see the fruit of my labor! Often times we work harder for others and give very little effort to our own dreams, ideas and purpose. God spoke to Joshua in Joshua 1:8 and told him he would have to make **his way** prosperous and then he would have good success. He also gave Joshua a formula.

*Joshua 1:8* – This book of the law shall not depart out of thy mouth; but thou shalt "meditate" therein day and night, that thou mayest "observe to do" according to all that is written therein: for then thou shalt make thy way prosperous, and then "thou shalt have" good success.

God gave Joshua a formula and it will work for us as well. Success does not just happen. It takes remembering God, diligence, commitment, focus, time, energy, effort, and self-discipline. You must be willing to follow through with your dream even if others do not believe you are capable. You must believe and keep believing until the vision comes to fruition. You don't have to wait until you have all the money to get started. Use what you have! You don't have to know all the details to get started. Just get started!

A great hindrance to achieving is measuring your

success against someone else's success. This is a sure way to get off track. There is always someone who can do it better. There is always someone who can do it faster. When you compare yourself to others you set yourself up for failure. My husband often tells a story about Bishop T.D. Jakes. We were reading something and found out Bishop Jakes and his wife were married on the same day and year as us. We are all about the same age. We are all in ministry. Bishop Jakes' ministry has grown tremendously, and ours not nearly as much. We know we have worked just as hard in ministry and have just as many testimonies of overcoming but we don't have thousands flocking to our church. My husband says if he compared our ministry to Bishop Jakes' ministry, he could cry every day. (Lol) He said he's going to keep doing what God has told him to do and receive the success God has given him. In other words, he is going to stay focused and continue fulfilling the will of God for his life.

A word of encouragement to you today is "You can!" Others have, and you can too! You can overcome every obstacle! You can overcome every hindrance! You can write that book! You can start that business! You can start that ministry! You can go on that trip! You can lose weight! You can eat healthier! You can! You can! You can do all things through Christ who strengthens you. (Philippians 4:13) Get busy! Get to work so someone can see your good works and glorify the Father which is in heaven!" (Matthew 5:16)

You Can Do It Too!

# Prophetic Word

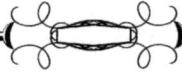

Thus saith the Lord, You can do it too. I have placed seeds of greatness inside of you. Each seed represents possibility. It is possible for you to do what you've been dreaming of, saith God. It is possible for you to be who you dreamed you could be. You *can* be an author! You *can* own your own business! You can! You can! Those dreams will manifest through nurturing your seeds. Each seed is nurtured when you begin to Do! Doing nothing causes the seeds to lie dormant. Many have died with unused seeds on their inside. Do not let this be you, saith God. Utilize every seed I have given you. The seeds are not just for you; as you begin to use them you will touch the lives of many. The more you *DO*, the more the seed will blossom causing greatness to manifest in your life. No one is greater than you, they just nurtured their seeds. Nurture your seeds, saith God. This is your time so don't let it pass you by. No more excuses! No more delays! Nurture your seeds, saith the Lord thy God!

# Power Scriptures

### Philippians 4:13
I can do all things through Christ which strengtheneth me.

### Proverbs 3:5-6
Trust in the Lord with all thine heart, and lean not unto thine own understanding. In all thy ways acknowledge him, and he shall direct thy paths.

### II Corinthians 5:7
For we walk by faith and not by sight.

### James 1:2-4
My brethren count it all joy when ye fall into divers temptations; (many trials) Knowing this, that the trying of your faith worketh patience. But let patience have her perfect work, that ye may be perfect and entire, wanting nothing.

### Isaiah 26:3-4
Thou wilt keep him in perfect peace, whose mind is stayed on thee: because he trusteth in thee. Trust in the Lord for ever: for in the Lord Jehovah is everlasting strength.

## Philippians 1:6

Being confident of this very thing, that he which hath begun a good work in you will perform it until the day of Jesus Christ.

## Psalm 37:4

Delight thyself also in the Lord, and he shall give thee the desires of thine heart.

## I Corinthians 15:58

Therefore, my beloved brethren, be ye stedfast, unmovable, always abounding in the work of the Lord, forasmuch as ye know that your labour is not in vain in the Lord.

## Proverbs 16:3

Commit thy works unto the Lord, and thy thoughts shall be established.

## Genesis 1:26-27

And God said, Let us make man in or own image, after our likeness: and let them have dominion over the fish of the sea, and over the fowl of the air, and over the cattle, and over all the earth, and over every creeping thing that creepeth upon the earth. So God created man in his own image, in the image of God created he him; male and female created he them.

# Reflections/Notes

# *Prayer of Salvation*

This book is all about empowerment through Jesus Christ. If you have read this book and have not accepted Jesus as your Savior, I would like to present this opportunity to you. Salvation is for everyone according to **John 3:16 (NLT)**

For this is how God loved the world: He gave his one and only Son, so that *everyone* who believes in him will not perish but have eternal life.

God sent his Son to die for **you! You** are just that special. You can't earn salvation, it must be received by faith in Jesus. Let's look at **Romans 10:9 (ESV)**

If you confess with your mouth that Jesus is Lord and believe in your heart that God raised him from the dead, you will be saved.

Please pray the following prayer with me.

Lord, forgive me for my sins. I believe in Jesus. I believe Jesus is the Son of God, died on the cross, rose from the grave, and only through his name can I be saved. Come into my heart Lord Jesus. Save me now! Lord I thank you that I am saved. Help me do your will as I surrender my life to you, in the name of Jesus. Amen!

If you prayed this prayer you are now saved. A good first step to learning more about Jesus is through reading the book of

St. John. St. John is the fourth book of the Bible in the New Testament. This book focuses on who Jesus is. I pray as you read it you will get a true revelation of Jesus and develop a personal relationship with him. God bless you on this lifelong journey.

www.ingramcontent.com/pod-product-compliance
Lightning Source LLC
LaVergne TN
LVHW051244080426
835513LV00016B/1731